How to Remember Names

A Mentalist's Guide to Remembering the Names

(Learning Faster Remember More and Be More Productive)

Gerald Weaver

Published By **Phil Dawson**

Gerald Weaver

How to Remember Names: A Mentalist's Guide to Remembering the Names (Learning Faster Remember More and Be More Productive)

ISBN   978-1-988842-08-0

No part of this guidebook shall be reproduced in any form without permission in writing from the publisher except in the case of brief quotations embodied in critical articles or reviews.

Legal & Disclaimer

Table Of Contents

Chapter 1: What's In A Name?

Before you could respect the art of remembering unique humans's names, you want to first understand who you're. By that I mean, do you honestly apprehend who you're? You are not an twist of future. You are fearfully and wonderfully made, and God knew you before you had been in your mom's womb.

Every name consists of significance because your name tells a tale. Since the start of time, names have instructed testimonies. When we check any historical literature, we discover that human beings carried an identification that went with their name. For instance, the choice Abram way "Exalted Father".1 Later in his life, God gave Abram a modern call and called him "Abraham". Abraham method "Father of a Multitude", or "Father of Many Nations".2 And that is exactly the life that Abraham lived out, and his call contains on in the route of contemporary history.

In historic times, human beings moreover said their parents in the method of introducing themselves, and also within the case of being added with the aid of others. For instance, King David, earlier than he have become king of Israel became not acknowledged via the term "King". He changed into acknowledged with the beneficial useful resource of the call David, son of Jesse. Sometimes he is probably referred to as David, from the house of Jesse. This is vital due to the fact there have been likely a number of David's handy! But there could have been best one David, from the house of Jesse. When he become brought this way, it carried due to this. He wasn't simply David. He changed into David, son of Jesse.

This precept includes through to trendy instances, as we've got first and final names. Yes, occasionally humans have center names and multiple names amongst their first and remaining names; but, I need to popularity on the two names that virtually remember range. My name is Danny, which comes from the premise word, Daniel. Daniel approach "God is my pick out".Three In addition, my final name is critical as well. My final call is McDaniel, due to this "Son of Donald". Donald method "World Ruler"; consequently, my last call method "Son of World Ruler".Four Now, that's powerful! It have emerge as no longer an twist of fate that my names carry the ones particular meanings as it contributes to my identification, myself worth, and my price.

If you don't develop an appreciation for the because of this of names, you could no longer come to be a grasp of remembering human beings's names for the proper reasons. It all starts offevolved offevolved with you knowing exactly who you're and what your name manner. In all of my years of assembly people, I may additionally venture to mention that less than half of of of the people I meet have a clue what their name manner. I ask people all the time, anyplace I cross, in the event that they understand what their call manner. Most of the time, I get a horrible reaction.

It's as clean as going to a seek engine and looking up the that means of your first name, in addition to the that means of your closing call. Some assets are higher than others; but, they're all quite handy through the internet. Because of my non-public beliefs, I generally tend to search for the biblical because of this of names.

There are many one in every of a type sites to search for name meanings that could benefit you in this way. It's clearly easy!

Questions to ask yourself:

What does your first name suggest?

What does your closing call imply?

What story does your name inform?

WHY NAMES ARE IMPORTANT

Deep down, you probably understand precisely why names are critical. You comprehend precisely the manner it feels whilst a person is ignoring you due to the truth they do no longer recognize your call, or they have to recognize your call, however forgot. It seems as though they do no longer fee you as a person, specifically in case you actually met them. There are exceptions to this, which need to be commonplace experience. If you met a person a 12 months earlier and simply observed them again for the primary time, they'll now not consider your call. This isn't always a devaluing condition the least bit. One of the terrific subjects you could ever do is apprehend that they don't consider you and re-introduce your self as you greet them. Don't purpose them to undergo thru the obvious; the truth that they do not endure in thoughts your name. I will cowl this hassle a touch later.

There are multiple reasons why names are so essential. One motive is that your name carries a terrific which means that, as stated inside the previous financial disaster. Your call is the get entry to factor for someone analyzing you higher. Most human beings don't clearly apprehend the significance of this get admission to detail. Your call gadgets the tone for the verbal exchange, and your name is an vital a part of some component that transpires beyond in reality meeting someone and strolling in your manner.

Once you get a actual revelation of the importance of your name, your name will deliver greater authority as you begin to introduce yourself. There's some thing special approximately you without a doubt knowing the significance of your name and the way it affects the humans in whom you meet.

My partner and I absolutely have three sons, who're now adults. Their entire existence, they have been taught that they have been made to be set aside. We typically counseled them that they have been fearfully and splendidly made, and that they have got been McDaniels. We usually advised them what the selection "McDaniel" intended, and that they were every a "Son of World Ruler". We taught them what it simply supposed to keep the decision McDaniel, and they might normally be set apart.

As our sons have grown up, they preserve to appearance lower lower returned and observe the importance of those schooling. In reality, in reality 4 days previous to me writing this sentence, we had a family meeting that turned into known as collectively thru our oldest son. During that own family meeting, our boys and daughter-in-felony suggestions started out out to percent with each other what it purported to them to have this form of tight knit family. In the course of the talk, our youngest son, TJ (Tatum Jayce), commenced to inform our own family how super it's far been to be raised as a McDaniel. He performs university soccer, and he knowledgeable us that he sees so masses of his pals round him who do not understand who they sincerely are, nor do they have a clue in which they may be genuinely going. He stated the significance of ways he grow to be taught that he modified into a "McDaniel" and that he modified into "set aside". And he expressed his deep gratitude, in tears, as to the manner it has affected his existence in such hundreds of strategies that I can not begin to unique on this book.

Your name topics too! And, if you truely begin to preserve close this concept, you may appreciably enhance your functionality to bear in mind precise humans's names for a long term.

What you need to look at from this idea is that human beings's names are virtually akin to a key. If you want of their existence, you need to use the important factor properly. Keys open doors, and your capacity to keep in mind the names of others will come up with a whole new set of keys to fun relationships. If names are like keys, then names depend variety!

The problem with our manner of lifestyles in recent times is that we were programmed to be self focused; therefore, we don't be aware of the topics that certainly depend. Other humans depend! But the world has knowledgeable you and me that we are what actually subjects. This spills over into the complete relationship trouble. When we're centered on ourselves, it's far tough to be aware about the matters that rely, like remembering exceptional humans's names. In the following financial disaster, you will start to have a study the primary steps to turning into a draw close of names. More than that, you'll win human beings over right away! Every step that I educate is going to will let you win people over more fast and extra frequently.

Points to Remember:

Work on absolutely valuing different people's names, in addition to your non-public.

Decide to be someone who's aware about you're "set aside".

In all of my years, the assignment of "introducing yourself" has been a big part of my existence. I grew up in small towns within the Seventies and 1980s. Although my family had masses of sickness, my father modified into a absolutely top notch dad. He turn out to be a without a doubt incredible educate, instructor, and father. Like many of the kids in my generation, there were powerful codes of behavior that were expected of all and sundry that modified into not an person. Here are a number of the ones codes of behavior:

When you introduce your self, appearance the man or woman within the eyes

Shake their hand firmly

Respond to adults with "Yes Sir/No Sir" and "Yes Mam/No Mam"

Always deal with adults with the aid of way of pronouncing "Mr. Smith", "Mrs. Smith", or "Ms. Smith"

Always say "Please" and "Thank You"

Always say "Excuse Me" while essential

Always open the door for others to are available earlier than you (particularly for girls)

As critical as all of these things nonetheless are, on this e-book I need to reputation at the importance of introductions. Introductions are the whole lot! Although instances have modified, the way you introduce your self units the tone for any first-rate courting to boom. As you're about to look, it will additionally assist you undergo in mind names hundreds plenty less difficult.

If you want to apprehend the way to win pals and feature an impact on people, hold close the art work of introducing yourself like a champion every time you meet someone. Here's the way you do it. The first detail that you ought to research is which you want to slow down your mind at the same time as you are introducing yourself, or being introduced. Let's say that you are absolutely assembly one precise person. If I am assembly a person for the number one time, as I method them, I deliberately give up being concerned approximately everybody else spherical me. I moreover slow down my mind to now not be involved about the subsequent ten seconds past assembly that individual. The purpose for that is that I want to hobby completely on how I introduce myself thru listening carefully to the character in the the front of me. The subsequent step is to increase your hand and shake their hand firmly, and look them in the eye...usually!

One of the issues that arises whilst humans introduce themselves is that each parties may additionally moreover perform their advent at the equal time, and neither of you pay attention the opportunity one. Then, you cross about pretending that everything is ok and considered without a doubt one in every of two subjects display up. One problem that takes place is that you truly do some issue it takes to transport on from your brief assembly. The one of a type element that occurs is which you spend your entire time beating yourself up for not remembering their name, which impacts the value of your verbal exchange.

What you need to see in this example is how critical it is for this extra youthful guy to introduce himself via his first and final name. There are a million guys alongside with his first name; but, there aren't very many guys collectively with his first and final call. His father, being an NFL wonderful, paved the manner for his own family to have want in relationships. Everything his father labored for and completed is nullified whenever this more youthful guy doesn't acknowledge his family name. This younger guy didn't understand if I became broke or a billionaire. He didn't understand that his dad end up one in every of my all time favorite gamers. He didn't understand that I should possibly have had the power to provide him a completely unique feature in my organization that would pave the manner for his destiny. He didn't recognize the power of the essential issue he turned into maintaining; his family call.

So, getting again to introducing yourself, it is critical to usually introduce yourself with the aid of using your first and your very last call. This have to appear every unmarried time you introduce yourself. When a person is introducing themselves to me, and that they terrific tell me their first name, I do not permit skip in their hand. I will preserve right now to their hand and hold searching them in the eye. Sometimes they right away understand to inform me their ultimate call. At that second, I hold my handshake with them and repeat their name thru using pronouncing, "Hey John, it's excellent to meet you." If they don't lure on that I am searching their remaining call, I without delay ask them what their final name is, whilst despite the reality that having a grip on their hand. After they tell me, I then repeat their name and tell them it is first-class to satisfy them.

Now, at this point, you need to not hurry up the verbal exchange. Slow down! It normally doesn't bear in mind what is said over the following 10 seconds or so due to the fact it is also small speak. The key is to hold searching them in the attention and inform your self, "His call is John Sullivan. His call is John Sullivan. His name is John Sullivan." If you repeat their complete call to your head three times and recognition on that one detail, you'll be extraordinary. Now, you're organized in case you need to engage with John even greater. The next time you cope with him, you could use his first name in case you land up asking a question. If he asks you a question, you may want to reply with some issue like, "You recognize John…" and answer the question. When it comes to John's very last call, you can want to assess his ultimate name to your very very very own human computer, and see if there can be some life connection which you have already got through a chum or relative of John's. Sometimes someone's final name offers you thrilling topics that bring about exploratory conversations about every awesome's lives. This can carry you desire inside the courting, and it will in reality assist you recollect someone's call.

Any time which you cease a communication with a contemporary-day person, you may usually want to call them thru their call whilst you are getting ready to say good-bye. It can be as easy as, "Hey John, it have become in reality super to meet you in recent times and get to understand you." Every unmarried time you say their name, you may construct the band width on your thoughts to undergo in mind them the following time you note them. If it takes location to be someone that I actually need to recollect, I will repeat their call in my head more than one extra instances at some point of the day, as soon as I actually have left my meeting with them.

This can also appear a bit "antique college", or antiquated for the common person in our manner of lifestyles in recent times, however I am right here to tell you, you aren't referred to as to be common! You sold this e-book so as to don't forget people's names and emerge as more influential in the lives of various people. I choice you're taking this significantly, because it works. My accomplice and I in reality have built a sales and advertising agency from 0 - 250,000 people; volunteers for that count range. These are people which can go away you and forget about you at any second. We have raised three champion sons this manner. We have planted and led a church, having visible multitudes of lives modified in the method. We teach control development on a high degree, and we teach marriage and parenting thoughts in all varieties of arenas. Our existence function has been in human relationships, and you can't discover the coins for to skip this primary step in remembering someone's name.

Always introduce yourself thru your first and final name; constantly. And constantly attempt to find out what a person else's remaining call is as properly. It will serve you well, as you may see within the subsequent chapter.

Points to Remember:

All the "codes of conduct" are an vital part of becoming someone of have an effect on.

You have to sluggish your mind down as you prepare to introduce yourself.

It's important to continually keep direct eye contact at some stage in the advent.

Always discover a dignified manner to tug a person's last name out of them in a communique.

Last names can lead you into lasting conversations and lasting relationships.

Chapter 2: Remembering Multiple Names

Right right right here are few matters more amusing than to look at humans's reactions at the same time as you can paintings a room of people with the aid of understanding all in their names. Everyone in the room acknowledges your particular ability of understanding everybody's call. There are only some reasons why humans don't make the selection to do what you're doing; it truly is to make the effort to don't forget everybody's name. Three reasons are; laziness, selfishness, and shortage of intentionality. People are simply lazy! And they make excuses why they can not bear in mind awesome humans's names whilst the best excuses for not remembering are lousy excuses. The reason that I stated selfishness is due to the reality if you simply care about extraordinary human beings, their name is critical to you. And it's far vital enough to learn how to get intentional at remembering distinct people's names.

Here's where this ebook gets in reality exciting, due to the fact I am going to teach you ways smooth it's miles to don't forget the names of an entire room complete of people. When you input a setting in which there are a couple of human beings involved, you need to enter that setting with a thoughts-set that the maximum essential component should take region is on the manner to get to understand who the people are. You want to make all of us inside the room sense valuable, and the fantastic way to do this is to consider all of their names.

Last week, really prior to writing this e-book, Diane and I attended a network dinner and celebration. We did now not recognize whether or not it changed into going to be a small amassing or a big collecting due to the fact those unique pals have a very huge home and they have even had valet parking and a whole issuer catering frame of employees at distinct talents in their domestic. So, as we have been making equipped to visit the celebration, Diane and I reviewed the names of all of our buddies on our street. We quizzed each different on the names of each couple on our street, that have been twelve considered one of a kind couples. If you are going to attend a celebration in which you recognize some of the folks that can be attending, one of the fine subjects you could do is assessment everyone's name in advance than you ever cross. It truly takes a touch extra time and intentionality to perform this.

When we entered the house, we located out that the dinner and birthday celebration modified into no longer massive, however there have been couples who did not stay on our avenue. So, we gladly shook fingers, hugged, and greeted our pals, but my actual focus have turn out to be to slow down my mind to pay attention to the 2 new couples. The first couple walked up to us and that they each introduced themselves through their first and closing names. I did the equal with them, and I right away commenced out to replicate in my head, "His call is Phil and her name is Cathy. That's Phil and she is Cathy. He is Phil and she or he or he's Cathy." They were an older couple than us, probably around 70 years antique, so that they were very familiar with introducing themselves thru their first and final names. The subsequent couple modified right into a younger couple, and that they have got been split up in precise regions of the house. I met the husband first, and he knowledgeable me his name modified into Blake. I immediately started out to say in my mind, "His name is Blake. That's Phil and he or she or he is Cathy. That's Blake. This guy is Blake." Now, I'm no longer truly focused on one man or woman. I have to look again over and remind myself the names of the two certainly one of a type people simply so I don't virtually forget about them brief.

But wait, there's extra! Behind the bar become a greater younger lady who modified into dressed in provider body of employees garments. She have become our sole catering and business enterprise body of workers member of the night time time, and her name topics too. Her lifestyles subjects. If you need to win friends and impact lots of humans to your lifestyles, hired team of workers humans at a function aren't intended to stroll around and fake they don't exist. They are human beings, with an identification, with a coronary coronary heart, and with a future. This doesn't recommend that you are going to offer all the employed employees at a function you undevoted time and hobby, but it's crucial to apprehend what the setting is. In this putting, the numbers had been small, and he or she have become the only unmarried individual within the residence in the midst of some unique couples. I introduced myself to her and he or she or he or he did the same. Not great did I introduce myself, but I stayed there for a couple of minutes and connected with Jessica. Jessica became Taiwanese, and she or he recommended me her quick story and a few subjects approximately her existence. Meanwhile, I may additionally look over at Phil and Cathy and remind myself what their names were. Then I may also need to take a look at Blake and remind myself what his call end up.

When you are at abilities like this, you may use all varieties of strategies of movement to shop for you some time to test the room and repeat names for your head. While exclusive human beings are popularity round considering mindless subjects, you are constantly scanning the room and reminding yourself what different humans's names are. When you are at any form of characteristic, there are commonly get away moments that provide you with time to take a step once more, test the room, and consider names. It stages from bars, counters with appetizers, restrooms, bookshelves, artwork, decor, and masses of various topics. But you need to have break out moments to test the room and repeat names in your head as you be a part of names to faces.

In this putting I knew I needed to meet Blake's accomplice, Peyton, which I did. And I moreover wanted to tug Blake's final name out of him to look if there were one-of-a-kind strategies that we might be related in lifestyles. Sure enough, there has been a connection amongst us. Less than a yr within the beyond, his sports sports agent was in search of to get him linked to my son for a few harm healing remedy because of the reality he become an injured NFL soccer participant. I had spoken together with his agent approximately him and we were looking to get him help. As quick as we determined out this, his face lit up and our communique went to a whole new diploma of connection. The relaxation of the night, we spent numerous time speaking approximately him and his associate's new existence in marriage, football, restoration, his destiny, and how my son might be capable of assist in saving his profession. It all got here from the final call. But it began with me gaining knowledge of every body's first call, due to the truth they recognize being recognized via manner of their first call. By the manner, I recognized Jessica for my part whenever she got here round to pinnacle off my glass with water, or each time she waited on us at some point of the relaxation of the nighttime.

Now, that end up most effective a tale approximately me memorizing the names of 5 new people at a night meal that my wife and I attended; however, the principle works the identical manner no matter what putting you are in. You use this equal approach at church, at carrying activities together along with your kids, at events, at employer meetings, or any vicinity that places you spherical people.

A few months in the past, I became doing enterprise education for an partner of mine of their home. They had approximately twenty to 20 five precise people that confirmed up for the training. I simplest had met a number of the ones humans but all over again. Most of them, I changed into assembly for the primary time. The education become supposed to start at 7:30 p.M., so I knew that I needed to be ready via 7:00 p.M. To satisfy and greet new human beings. I might also moreover need to have acted like a film superstar and now not cared whether or not or now not I met any of these humans. I can also want to have absolutely expert them for 2 hours, like strangers, and predicted them to perform in enterprise. But that's no longer the manner you emerge as someone of honor and a person of have an effect on. As a pacesetter, you bypass the extra mile. If you need to make a difference in human beings's lives, you want to assume otherwise than the common man or woman thinks. I had to use the 1/2 of-hour preceding to the meeting to shake palms, greet people, have interaction in conversation, and hold in mind names.

When the number one individual or couple walked through the door I brought myself to them and went through my repeating manner in my thoughts. As the second one person or couple walked through the door, I did the equal problem. Then I began to copy all four names in my head as they had been speaking. I couldn't capture every single character on foot through the door; however, that's when you have to begin strolling on your other techniques of having to your self in short. In this case, I had the kitchen that I can also need to break out to. I may additionally need to say, "Excuse me, I ought to cross capture a drink of water." I had the rest room that I should use. I had the excuse that I desired to test on my

Apple TV tool, to ensure that it became going to feature well. And I really had the excuse of, "Excuse me, but I'm going to move in advance and attempt to meet a few more people earlier than the training begins offevolved."

As I worked the awesome rooms of the residence for thirty mins, which had been the lobby, ingesting room, kitchen, and living room, I endured to apply my approach of repeating names. For example, because the number of humans I met grew in variety, I should try to step again and take a look at the room. As I did, I may want to say in my thoughts, "That's Jerry, that's David, she's Margie, he's Ricky, she's Virginia, she's Teri, that female is Donna, her husband is Dave, that's Jason, she's Samantha, and so forth., and so on." What you want to do is generally take a look at the room and repeat humans's names on your head at the identical time as you hook up with their faces. It's truely smooth! It just takes a touch exercising.

Now, I will say that one approach that I utilized in this case have become to ask my host for the names of who all she had coming that night. So, she had been telling me names of people, however I did not have faces to connect to those names. But that little little bit of knowledge prior to them coming for the nighttime helped. I will cowl more on this in a later financial ruin.

At 7:30 or so, whilst we commenced out the training, I stepped up in the the front of the dwelling room complete of people and welcomed absolutely everyone. I stated the reason of the education and stated multiple more topics that led me into having the capability to name each one in every of them with the resource of name. It had a few factor to do with us analyzing each one of a kind and constructing don't forget. I then started out out to transport during the room and speak to each single individual within the room via way of their first call. They were blown away! They could not recollect that I surely rattled off twenty to twenty five superb names of humans without making one mistake. For me it have become easy. It emerge as only a depend of me understanding that the maximum essential trouble that I can do in a social situation is to consider people's names and understand them. It builds be given as actual with and deepens wholesome communication.

Overall, this is how you figure in a room with as few as three or 4 people, or a larger organisation of twenty human beings or more. It's all about eye touch, repeating names in your thoughts, asking questions about their call or remaining call, and escaping to find out moments to test the room and repeat names for your thoughts as you join faces to names. It's genuinely easy and a laugh!

Let's examine a putting in that you need to stroll into a commercial company assembly with some new human beings, and you land up shaking six human beings's fingers within the path of approximately thirty seconds. Hopefully, you introduce yourself thru the use of your first and final call, you appearance anyone in the eye with out hurrying, and also you repeat their name once they greet you. This doesn't assure that you'll be great and sit down down down for the meeting knowledge who anyone is. It become best a start. Here's what you do next. When you sit down down down for the assembly, you can speak up and say something like, "Hey! Before we get started out, I need to make sure that I without a doubt have everybody's call proper. So, you are Brenda, you are Brandon, you're Michael, you're Eva, and you are Shawna. Is that proper?" This isn't the appropriate sentence that you can use while you do this, but it's miles an example as to how you may technique it. If you've got forgotten one or of the names, as you look at them and probably aspect to them, in reality examine them which includes you're now not advantageous and perform the word "And yooouuu'rrre" in a question-like tone. They will straight away apprehend to country their call yet again, and also you each will smile and the whole lot may be virtually high-quality. But now you realise every person in the room. The next step is to write down their names in your notes right away due to the reality there's generally a risk that you could forget. You certainly have more reinforcement now.

We are in an business enterprise where we're capable of cross on some of vacations with huge corporations. In addition, we pass on assignment journeys with companies of human beings. On the ones events, it also includes first-class to have a virtual file of all of the names of attendees of the revel in, their images, wherein they may be from, and names in their children. You must in no manner bypass on a fixed adventure while not having preceding information of the attendees, with some manner of reading their names and faces previous to the adventure.

As I am penning this e-book, my spouse and I are principal a set of 50 people to a seaside excursion marriage convention. We are the usage of a Facebook organization for these couples to location their picture and their family records in a thread so that each one of the alternative couples can begin to be a part of names to faces. Why would possibly we allow all of them to truely display as much as the convention without giving them a headstart on reading every different? I want you to start to think like this from this component ahead.

In the following chapters, I will offer you with a few extra guidelines a good way to appreciably help you put together for any new introductions. It may be a single creation or a couple of introductions in a fixed placing, however there are a few realistic and easy hints that absolutely everyone can use to endure in thoughts human beings's names less complicated.

Points to Remember:

In a set placing, interest on the modern day human beings inside the room.

Slow down your idea technique just so your number one consciousness is names and faces.

Learn the manner to exercise scanning the room and repeating names.

Practice your brief escape methods to find out time to test the room.

Chapter 3: Know Where You Are Going!

Right right here are times while we without a doubt do now not understand what to expect whilst we input a certain room. Every situation is special, and there can be no superb answer for making geared up earlier for assembly people. However, there are usually that you have hundreds of opportunities to perform a touch homework in advance of time earlier than you input right into a placing in which your reminiscence might be challenged.

Here's one of the first subjects that I do if I am going to a place that is hosted through someone. If I am near with the host, I will ask who is attending. If I am going to a business commercial enterprise business enterprise event and I am speaking, I can also ask for a list of names of attendees in order that I can take a look at over the names of the attendees. Obviously, in a really big commercial company assembly or ministry event, I might also need to no longer be doing this. But you ought to be able to apprehend what I am talking approximately. I do a number of ministry sports. If I get invited to a ministry event or a retreat, I will ask for a listing of names of the registrants simply so I can pray for them each day previous to the event. This permits me to sincerely get their names in my head because I am each reading their names from a list every day, and I am calling their names out in prayer. When I meet them in character, I can start to be a part of faces to names right away. In most times, human beings in ministry don't introduce themselves thru their first and remaining names anymore, so I already recognize their final call. This sincerely blows them away. For instance, a girl can also furthermore stroll as much as me and introduce herself as Sandra. And I will say, "Hey are you Sandra Brown?" And she could be capable of immediately slight up with a smile and say, "Yes! How did you recognize that?" And it lets in our conversation to be hundreds more meaningful.

Finding out the names of human beings in whom you may be with previous to any characteristic will extensively lessen the mastering curve with regards to getting to know the names of the human beings to your midst. I in no way make it awkward for a number of. I don't have a few bizarre wishes that make human beings flip over names or supply me lists. I in reality examine most situations that I am making prepared to go into. And, if there can be a manner for me to get a headstart on remembering names, I will take gain of it.

Social media may be used as an splendid tool that will help you undergo in mind names and join names to faces. If I apprehend that positive people are going to be in a placing that I want to make an awesome affect with, I will visit social media to attempt to find out more approximately them. Just by using way of scrolling via someone's social media, you begin to construct a reminiscence that makes it easy as a manner to join their call to their face at the same time as you sincerely meet them in individual. This idea is really simple and it doesn't require quite some education. You surely need to apprehend that it's miles a tool with the intention to permit you to recall people's names; consequently, you can need to take advantage of it.

When I am going places, I will always ask the host, "Who do I actually need to get to apprehend?" Or, "Who do you really need me to apprehend that is coming?" Upon asking this kind of questions, I can get centered on remembering the key human beings in whom they actually need me to hook up with. What I can also do at that detail is try to look them up on social media, or have my buddy display me who they'll be on social media. Now, I have already got their names and faces logged into my thoughts after I meet them, so it gives me a memory benefit when I meet them for the primary time.

Points to Remember:

Always think about who's going to be wherein you are, prior to arriving.

Use social media and the expertise of friends to aid your memory.

Chapter 4: Searching Name Meanings

One of the topics that has helped me immensely with remembering humans's names, is to become familiar with the meanings of other human beings's names. Not great does it assist me don't forget humans's names and faces better, but it absolutely has a strong impact on human beings's lives.

I love to ask new humans in whom I meet what their name technique. Sometimes they understand what their name manner and it will become a really splendid communication. Most of the time, they don't realise what their call technique in any respect, so we look it up on the net proper there. When I check to them what their name method, they mild up with a smile and all forms of high-quality topics appear to show up in the ones conversations.

I regularly ask the man or woman at the checkout counter of a industrial organisation popularity quo what their name method. If they don't recognize, I will tell them and feature a great time the that means in their name with them. If I don't realise what their name technique, I will look it up on the same time as they may be taking me via the take a look at out method. The same holds real once I am eating at a restaurant and I ask the waiter or waitress what his or her call is. I particularly bear in mind one time asking a waitress what her name changed into and she or he replied, "It's Isabella." I then responded, "Oh, Isabella. I like that. Do you understand what Isabella way?" She did now not recognize so I informed her, "It technique 'Pledged from God'. You are a present from God, and that is this kind of beautiful call." You can take into account what her reaction grow to be at that aspect. It became a very unique 2nd for her, and she or he or he felt valued. I in fact have loads of those recollections.

This exercising is really a few factor that I do all of the time. I like to apprehend what human beings's names imply, and I believe it facilitates me connect to human beings on a far deeper degree. I bear in thoughts that it helps me benefit select with humans, and I be given as authentic with that it builds accept as true with. People want to feel valued, and exploring the meaning in their call with them simply adds price to their existence. And, it significantly complements your capability to keep in mind people's names.

Last names are critical as properly. People's closing names can take you into an entire new direction of communique. I use humans's ultimate names to talk about what part of the arena they might be from, or what part of the sector their ancestors came from. In America, we live in a melting pot; therefore, there are humans from all over the global that live everywhere in the america. If you take observe of humans's final names, you turns into lots greater talented at remembering names and gaining impact with human beings. When I meet someone who tells me their first and very last call and they appear to have roots overseas, I will constantly discover that during conversation. For instance, I would likely meet someone with an African call, and I understand that it's far surely Kenyan. I will ask, "That is a Kenyan call, isn't it?" And they may reply with a powerful "Yes" and question me how I knew that. Most of the time they'll right away query me if I've been there. This, in turn, ends in extremely good verbal exchange and permits me consider this man or woman's name a good buy higher. The equal way holds actual for any African united states of the us, South America, Europe, or Asia. When you get correct at this, you can select out their u . S . A . Of foundation with a very excessive fulfillment rate, and people love the reality that you care enough to ask them approximately their ethnicity and their roots.

I want to write story after tale after story of the remarkable conversations that I sincerely have with people from one of a type ethnicities who certainly are delighted as soon as I apprehend wherein they or their circle of relatives comes from. It ends in conversations approximately their food, their u . S ., their manner of life, and things like that. And whilst you could't understand exactly wherein they may be from, maximum of the time, they discover it impossible to resist at the same time as you wager. They will in reality ask you to bet in which their final name comes from, with a large smile on their face.

The extra that you practice this, the better you'll get at faces as properly. People from almost each u.S. Inside the worldwide have high quality facial tendencies that you may start to pick out up on in case you start to workout introducing your self together together with your first and ultimate call, and make the effort to get their first and last name. I even have come to be to the aspect in which I can tell the distinction amongst a person from Thailand and a person from Viet Nam. I can tell the difference among someone from Korea as opposed to a person from China. I can inform the difference among someone from Nigeria and someone from Kenya, or the Congo, or Uganda. I can tell the difference among someone from Brazil and a person from Mexico or Central America. It simply takes exercise, and this exercise permits your functionality to recollect each names and faces.

Another essential a part of remembering names and gaining have an effect on with people is to get their call proper. If you are meeting someone for the primary time and also you don't understand the way to pronounce their name effectively, permit them that will help you. They will sincerely respect you, and you can do not forget their name lots less difficult. Do no longer be afraid to invite for assist announcing a person's call. You might also commentary to them that it's miles a "honestly particular" call or a "really beautiful" call, and ask them what the tale is inside the back of their call. But maximum of all, do not introduce yourself to someone and muddle via trying to find to pronounce their name if you enjoy such as you in all likelihood did no longer pay attention it successfully. Ask for assist.

There are Chinese medical doctors that presently live in the course of the cul-de-sac from me, and their names had been initially a bit hard to pronounce. When we first met them at a neighborhood collecting, I asked the husband to replicate his name several times as I practiced it. He simply favored it and we have got emerge as buddies. Let me repeat myself. He appreciated me education his call proper in the the front of him as it commemorated him that I preferred to pronounce his call effectively. I do the identical trouble once I meet Asians at a nail salon or spa. When I understand for a reality that their call is not "Tina", I will ask them what their real call is. They love this, especially if you may take time to pronounce it efficiently once more to them and greet them well. When you leave the spa or nail salon an hour later and tell them good-bye via the usage of their real call, they may be very stimulated. It makes human beings enjoy valued.

This even works with folks that are natives of your very own u.S.. Here inside the United States, I will be aware of peoples' dialects, similarly to examine their facial look, clothing, and hair fashion. This gives me clues as to what state they may be from; therefore, I will use these clues to interact them and get to recognize them higher. You can memorize records which includes names all day lengthy, but if you don't have a motive for doing so, the memorization does no longer don't forget. It's all approximately the relationship that develops from step one in every of remembering someone's call.

Also, make certain that people pronounce your call effectively. If a person calls me "Daniel", I will surely allow them to recognize my call is "Danny", now not "Daniel". They appreciate it and we get subjects squared away. If a person calls you with the useful resource of using a totally notable call because of the reality they were given you combined up with each unique individual, then accurate them. They should need you to correct them. Don't simply smile at them and anticipate to your self, "Wow, this man is looking me a person else...horrible man doesn't maintain in mind my name." No! Help her or him out with the useful aid of correcting them. After all, your name honestly topics, so don't permit human beings call you with the resource of some other name even through twist of destiny.

There are instances at the identical time as absolutely everyone call a person with the useful resource of the incorrect call, and there are many motives for it. Sometimes, someone has a face this is similar to someone else you understand or have mentioned on your lifestyles, and also you wind up getting their name combined up with the character you are in the front of. Sometimes, there are in reality names which may be exceedingly comparable in how they're stated and also you wind up questioning their call is some element actually one of a type than what they informed you after they delivered themselves. Sometimes, your communique reasons you to reflect onconsideration on or communicate about someone else, and now that call is on the main edge of your thoughts. In flip, you can name the person you're speakme with by means of the wrong call. It's proper enough. Just apologize and make certain which you do get their call successfully thereafter. The super manner to decorate that is to replicate their name at the least 3 times on your thoughts as you're interacting with them.

Points To Remember:

Become talented at the usage of net net web sites to drag up meanings of names.

Pay interest to humans's remaining name spelling and which means.

Pay hobby to humans's facial talents, garments, and hair patterns for clues.

Pronounce humans's names efficaciously and do no longer make excuses.

Chapter 5: I Forgot Their Name!

One people are exempt from the reality that we every so often can not hold in mind a person's name in whom we have have been given met. This may be a person that we absolutely met ten seconds inside the past, or someone that we met according to week within the beyond, or perhaps several months inside the past. We all run into situations that purpose us to fast panic because of the reality we can't go through in mind someone else's call. I am going to offer you with some insights that I agree with are big in the region of studying the easy artwork of remembering names and faces.

The first example of forgetting names occurs whilst we introduce ourselves to a person, but we don't surely cognizance on being attentive to the opportunity individual usa their call. It occurs to us all. It certainly method that you approached that creation with distractive mind. You need to paintings to get rid of distractive mind; however, while it does show up, there's an clean way to triumph over the mistake. It's referred to as, "Please forgive me, tell me what your call is once more." It's as easy as this! Most human beings received't do that due to the truth they sense embarrassed or scared that it will make a horrible effect. The fact is that now not doing that's what makes a awful have an impact on. The motive why is due to the truth that person can be capable to inform because the verbal exchange flows which you haven't any clue what their name is anymore. I can display this via reminding you that you continuously realize at the identical time as you're talking with someone whether they recollect your name or not. Because you may tell that they don't recollect who you're, it influences your communication. And it specifically reveals itself at the surrender of the verbal exchange while you begin to play the complete "It modified into so incredible to fulfill you" recreation. This is an change of floor level feedback that humans make closer to each extraordinary whilst they may be in search of to exit a verbal exchange with whom they do no longer don't forget the alternative character's name.

The faster that you widely recognized which you did not bear in mind someone's name, the higher. Sometimes you could say a few words apart from, "I'm sorry, however what is your name over again?" It's proper sufficient to let them understand that you got harassed, and it's nicely sufficient to even say the way you wound up now not taking images their name. Sometimes you meet human beings with a name like "Jessica", but you start to assume her call is "Jennifer". There are numerous call similarities that could reason you to adventure up on remembering a name in the first ten seconds of an creation. The key's on the way to begin to stretch your self and be accurate enough with asking a person what their call is all over again. Just bear in mind your self. When you meet a person and a few seconds later they ask you what your call is once more, do you get indignant? No! No one receives offended. You honestly appreciate the fact that they cared sufficient to invite you all over again virtually so they may interact in a great communique with you. Therefore, if that is honestly genuine, then you certainly need to inspire your self to step out and do this element that you suppose is tough, but it is in reality now not tough. It will help you win extra pals and have an effect on extra people.

Let's say this doesn't occur, and one way or the opposite sooner or later of the verbal exchange you forgot their name. It's nevertheless ok to invite them on the stop of the verbal exchange, "Hey! I'm sorry, however what is your first name once more? I didn't do a remarkable approach listening at the equal time as you counseled me the primary time." They will recognize you asking them. You don't need to cease your conversation with the conventional semi-fake smiles and ground "it grow to be so quality to meet you" remark.

Also, do now not inform human beings which you are horrible with names. This is a terrible excuse. You are not terrible with names. How frequently do you concentrate humans say, "I'm so horrible with names"? You pay interest it all of the time and it's miles just a willing excuse for now not honestly being involved about the coronary heart of a few different individual. When you start to seize the essence of coronary coronary heart to coronary coronary heart conversation and communication, your international of remembering names will trade all the time.

There are special opportunity techniques of capturing someone's call that will help you keep in mind them at the same time as you neglect. One of those is social media, as I stated earlier. Social media is likewise a exquisite device that will help you recollect the names of human beings's kids.

Another technique is easy name affiliation. When you meet a "Jennifer", it's miles beneficial to attempt to image a few exceptional "Jennifer" in whom you comprehend and companion the 2 names collectively. This may also moreover assist you preserve from getting burdened and calling her "Jessica". This call association can be used with any call that you are running hard to undergo in thoughts as you join names to faces.

One of the ways that facilitates me don't forget some humans's names better is how I input names in my cellular telephone. When I meet a person and land up putting his contact information in my cellphone, I positioned his partner's call in the 1/three placement spot (enterprise agency) on my smartphone absolutely beneath his final call. I may also even enter all of their children' names and some time in the notes section of my mobile phone. I used to pastor a church, and it changed into crucial for me to recognize all of the people of every own family in my church, so I often had their entire circle of relatives in the notes section of in fact all of us's cellular phone variety.

There are instances at the same time as you can use your smartphone to alternate numbers, and it's going to assist you hold in thoughts one's name. Depending at the manner you finesse your manner into getting their call effectively in your touch base, this option let you win with human beings. Sometimes, you can open up your touch listing and hand them your cellphone and say, "Hey, permit's stay related. Can you fill it in and I will textual content you so that you can have my range too?" This is an easy manner to get a person's final name as properly, whilst you both hand them your cellular smartphone, or you fill their name in your self.

Another way that will help you recall names is for the humans which are close to you to be aware of how they may allow you to out. Sometimes you discover your self moving into a setting in which you understand that brilliant humans are going to be in the room, however you in reality can't undergo in mind their name. I work the friend system with my close buddies. I will tell my buddy that I need his help thru strolling as lots as "outstanding" humans first and introducing himself so that I will pay attention them repeat their name. Then I will step in next and greet them thru their first name due to the fact I had formerly met them.

The friend device works quite properly if you communicate thru taken into consideration certainly one of a type eventualities collectively in conjunction with your friend in advance than entering into social settings. My friend is aware of that if I need assist with a call, they may make sure and walk up to me within the center of my conversation and discover a way to name that character thru their first name. With all of my buddies, I make it a challenge to have a have a look at them in conversation and be conscious if they're suffering with first names. Not understanding a person's name is one of the best topics to perceive amidst conversations with people. You surely have to start noticing, and you can help your pals out. In flip, you have to teach your pals how to help you as well.

Another key way to assist someone who has likely forgotten a call is to play the arrival endeavor. When I am greeting someone on the facet of a pal, if I understand the man or woman, I may be extra assertive and technique that person first. After I greet them, I can also say, "Chris, you understand my buddy Dusty don't you?" In this case, I in reality helped every Chris and Dusty. Both of them would possibly have preferred help remembering the other person's call. This identical tactic applies to couples.

Sometimes it is my buddy main the manner for me after a greeting. For instance, if me and my spouse are in a social setting on foot with two of our near friends, they will take the lead on greeting every other couple. As quickly as they greet them, they may ask that couple, "Hey Ronnie and Sharon, have you ever met the McDaniels?" If we've, then our friends simply helped us make more potent remembering "Ronnie" and "Sharon's" names. When you're around influential leaders, you can word that they workout this quite often. This is one of the methods to help you consider names, win friends, and effect people.

There are activities at the identical time as you run into a person in public whom you understand, but you cannot remember their call and it insects you the whole time you're talking to them. These conversations constantly start with, "Hey, it's so accurate to peer you! How have you ever ever ever been?" Immediately the other man or woman is aware about which you do not preserve in thoughts their name. Trust me, it's far pretty obvious. You are aware about it and that they realise it. So, most of the time humans simply play alongside and act like the whole lot's perfectly ok. However, those conversations are crippled thru the brutal reality that the complete time you are speakme, you're rattled with the useful resource of way of the reality that you don't keep in thoughts their call. Here's how you could deal with this problem.

The first detail which you can do is say, "Hey it's first-rate to look you! I'm sorry, I absolutely realise your call however I'm having a brief mind lapse." Or you can say, "Hey, it's so super to appearance you. I'm form of embarrassed because I understand exactly who you are, but my mind is short circuiting proper now, so need to you help me out?" And once they respond to you and offer you with their call, you allow them to understand how appreciative you are, but don't stay on it. Just float on and be personable. It takes place to the top notch mother and father, whether or not or not it's miles on the grocery keep, the ballgame, or the airport.

In reality, allow me allow you to recognise a story about a top notch couple we ran into at an airport after having no longer seen them for more than one years. We knew them from a business enterprise that we had been each involved with, and we have been on severa corporation vacations with them as nicely. I remembered the husband's call proper away, however I simply couldn't don't forget the spouse's call. As I stood there and struggled to tug it up in my thoughts, I virtually had to break the communication and ask her what her first call turned into. I said some factor very close to, "Hey, you gotta tell me your first call another time. I don't recognise why I'm having a brain block however I am honestly not firing on all cylinders nowadays." She then suggested me her call. I apologized that I had to be reminded and we moved on in communication for a few different 5 minutes or so earlier than anyone headed to our gate connections. Since then, we started out interacting greater regularly on social media with every one in all a kind.

Just some days previous to writing this e-book, I come to be on the grocery preserve and bumped into a mom and her son whom I've identified for over ten years. The son became a young man that I coached whilst he modified into in immoderate school and knew him nicely because of the truth he moreover attended our church from the first day that we installed it. The mom come to be a person that I were given to apprehend nicely at the identical time as she and her husband commenced attending the church that we hooked up. I don't pastor that church anymore, and that they don't attend that church, so I haven't seen them in over years. As I end up taking walks through them within the grocery keep, I genuinely didn't see them surely due to the fact I changed into looking for as though I "had been on a undertaking". As I exceeded thru the usage of them with a brief look I just caught a glimpse of her face, however it changed into sufficient for me to save you and flip spherical. I recalled the son's call right now; however, for the lifestyles of me I could not don't forget the mother's name. So, my on the spot response have become to mention, "Wow, it's the Andersons! It's fantastic to see you!" So, the best facts is that I addressed them through manner of their circle of relatives call and commenced to speak. Within the following 60 seconds or so, I ultimately recalled her call and I wound up weaving her first name into the communication. Of route, at the prevent of the conversation I additionally informed them good-bye through addressing each of them through way in their first names. You, too, can get innovative collectively along with your restoration techniques! It in reality takes intentional practice.

A bonus tip on winning buddies and influencing humans is to recognize the importance of name tags that employees put on inside the service commercial enterprise company. They placed on the ones name tags for a motive; so you don't should ask them what their call is. Consequently, you have to generally make an effort to deal with any and each worker you interact with through the decision this is on their call tag. Whether it is on the the front of your interaction with them or it's far a clean, "Thank you Gracie! Have a high-quality day", it is important if you want to apprehend them thru name. Name tags recollect. But it is the individual within the lower back of the call tag that virtually topics! There is a famous law of sowing and reaping. As you sow, so shall you advantage; therefore, what you do in thriller via spotting human beings will come over again to you in distinct regions of your lifestyles.

In end, I need to inform you that you may honestly hold near the art work of remembering names and faces of human beings. You have the capacity to endure in mind all and sundry's call. You have 3 million years properly absolutely well worth of garage ability on your brain; therefore, there can be no motive why you have to not be able to draw close the art work of remembering human beings's names. There are over four billion actions per 2d taking location on your brain each 2d, however you are high-quality conscious of thousand of them. Take gain of these thousand thoughts in keeping with second. When you appearance human beings in the attention to meet them, I need you to slow down and recognition on the choice. Just reputation on the call. Pay attention to what they're saying. Don't appearance to the right or to the left. Focus mostly on the character inside the the front of you and do not hurry to the following person. Repeat their call in your head earlier than you skip immediately to the following man or woman.

I would like as a way to consider names in a whole one-of-a-kind manner. I need to have written a e-book about all types of little intellectual hints and funny connections among a person's name and animals. There are some of mnemonic gadgets that will let you hold in thoughts names. There are such a lot of extremely good little techniques that it can probable weigh down you to ought to depend on them. I want to keep topics clean and realistic. What I definitely have laid out for you works and it is confirmed. But you need to understand that it is not the stop all. It is simply my manner of coaching because I like for human beings as a way to maintain topics simple. The hard element is in untraining your thoughts from the concern, guilt, and embarrassment of feeling along with you don't recognize what to do at the same time as you could't go through in mind someone's call after having met them. You need to maintain the mind-set that it is flawlessly and socially appropriate to mention:

"I'm sorry, however…"

"I forgot…"

"Can you tell me your name another time?"

"Forgive me, but…"

Every person in whom you come across in lifestyles is vital enough to at least widely recognized them via the use of their first call. If you start to exercise the ones strategies on a normal basis, it's going to profoundly change your life. You might be known as someone who truly cares. You may be called someone of have an effect on. You will trap essential relationships on your life plenty much less complicated. The blessings are severa, but most of all, you may have the joy of information that the seemingly little contact that you made on someone's existence come to be not a touch contact the least bit. It impacted them appreciably. These little touches compound, and that they turn out to be a amazing harvest. So press in and pay close to interest to all which you have located out. Apply this new expertise and records and watch your self turn out to be a primary have an effect on upon the lives of others.

Points To Remember:

If you neglect someone's name…don't wait…short ask them once more.

Never make excuses which you are horrible at names.

Learn to work with friends to help every one of a kind out.

If an employee is sporting a call tag, cope with them in my opinion.

Chapter 6: The 3 Causes Of Forget-Ory

That's accurate. If you don't get the call efficaciously inside the first area, there's no way to keep in mind it. Or, in exceptional terms… If you don't GET it, you may't KEEP it.

Sometimes you didn't pay attention the character say their name. Or, likely the character has an unusual sounding call that you're not familiar with.

Many times an introduction will move something like this…

"Joe, I'd which includes you to fulfill my friend Mr. Blblblb." And, perhaps Joe will say , "Hi. How are you doing?" (Never having gotten the man's name.)

The Second Cause Of "Forget-ory"… YOU DON'T CARE.

Now, I understand that perhaps saying which you don't care may also additionally moreover sound a bit callous. But, what takes location is that on occasion, we're so concerned with telling folks who WE are, that we virtually aren't paying any interest to who THEY are.

Sometimes our hobby gets distracted. Here you are assembly this fellow over proper here and mentally you're questioning some thing like: "Nice in form he's wearing. I wonder what it value." Or, as you're shaking hands with someone new at a party, your mind is probably wandering, and thinking some thing like, "wherein's the meals"? (Have you ever stuck your self doing that?)

Did your Mom ever say a few detail like this to you at the same time as you had forgotten to perform a little element you have got got been imagined to do for her… "You can first-class recall what you WANT to keep in mind." Well, she modified into proper!

Did you ever word which you have a remarkable reminiscence for some matters but no longer for others? Maybe you're high-quality at sports sports activities information. Or possibly you're suitable at details about film stars. It's much less difficult to recollect matters that hobby you, isn't it?

So, likely your reminiscence isn't as lousy as you perception, huh? You sincerely need to need to bear in mind someone's call badly enough to surely DO some thing approximately it. (Like observe the great-powerful strategies provided right here.)

The Third Cause Of "Forget-ory"… YOU DON'T BELIEVE.

The first two reasons of "Forget-ory" are quite small in evaluation to this one. This is the 'Biggie'! It's which you don't believe you have got already had been given an amazing reminiscence for human beings's names (Or some thing else, for that depend).

Have you ever used expressions like the ones?

"I can constantly remember a face, however, I can never take into account a call."

" I truly have a awful memory"

"Oh, I should be developing vintage. I can't appear to preserve in mind things anymore."

"I need to be getting Alzheimer's illness." (Meantime, you're like best to your 20's or 30's.)

I've even heard humans, searching for to be humorous, say some thing like: "I usually overlook a face, however, I in no manner endure in mind a name."

Saying the ones types of topics to your self isn't the quit result of a terrible memory.

It is the cause!

Telling your self that your memory will fail you isn't always a few element more than a self-fun prophecy. You make it real, due to the fact you consider it to be authentic.

It works like this: if you receive as authentic with you have got have been given a awful memory now, why need to you even try and do not forget someone's name. After all, you've got a awful memory, proper? You're already beat earlier than you start. And, who's beating you? That's proper, you're beating your self.

Now, the answer isn't to abruptly start pronouncing subjects to your self like: "Oh my memory is right now." Your past experience will negate that belief. A 2d later you'll say to yourself, "Oh, positive! That's fun."

No. The accurate manner of converting your thinking pattern may be cited in element a piece later in this path. You'll observe as soon as and for all, exactly what to tell your self as a way to pressure your memory to emerge as sturdy and reliable.

Your mind is a mechanism. It will observe some issue orders you supply it. If you inform it which you have a lousy reminiscence, it's going to take delivery of as real with you. It will supply a susceptible reminiscence. However, if you study the right manner to well inform it how effective and effective your memory is… it will obey you, and provide an exquisite memory you can rely on.

AN OLD DOG WHO WILL TEACH US NEW TRICKS!

The strategies and strategies we're going employ in this software are not new. Far from it!

As a count of reality, they date back to historic times. Specialized memory strategies are called mnemonics (referred to with a silent 'M': nee MON icks). They are named after the Greek Goddess of reminiscence: Mnemonsyne (nih MON sin ee).

One of the maximum well-known of the early practitioners of mnemonics, became someone named Simonedes (sih MON eh deez).

Simonedes come to be said to have had the world's great memory, on the time he changed into alive. He emerge as famous for performing some first rate feats of mental energy. For example he is stated to had been succesful to name with the resource of call nearly each inhabitant of historic Athens.

That have come to be about 30,000 people!

You are approximately to examine the suitable equal strategies correctly used for loads of years, through way of infinite generations, to provide you, an exquisite reminiscence for names.

ALLOW ME TO INTRODUCE YOU

What's step one in assembly a person? Correct... the advent. This is in which most humans blow it. There are multiple very not unusual errors which are regularly made at some point of the advent.

Let's take a look at an average creation and be aware what is going incorrect. Then, thru expertise the issues, you may be capable to overcome them.

A common introduction regularly goes like this.

Host: "Joe, I'd consisting of you to meet my pal Mary."

Joe: "Hi. How are you?"

Mary: "Hello. Nice to satisfy you."

That sounds OK, proper?

Did you capture the massive mistake that each Joe and Mary every made?

The problem is that neither Joe nor Mary used every special's name while meeting.

Here's the manner it want to be achieved.

Host:"Joe, I'd together with you to fulfill my buddy Mary."

Joe:"Hi MARY. How are you?"

Mary:"Hello JOE. Nice to satisfy you?"

Here's each other commonplace trouble.

Sometimes, the person making the introductions will mumble the decision of the man or woman being delivered, or the man or woman may want to have a foreign places or an uncommon sounding call. In each case, in case you aren't positive what a person's name is, ask them to copy it. It's as easy as that.

What in case you're nevertheless no longer sure about the call? A accurate solution is to invite the person how it is spelled. By spelling the name, it will offer you with a less attackable draw close to of it. It makes it much less complicated to visualize.

Don't ever be embarrassed approximately asking a person to copy their name or to spell it for you. Usually, they may be thrilled and flattered that you are taking an hobby in them. People need you to go through in thoughts them.

Overcoming 2 out of three

Remember the three Causes Of "Forget-ory"?

(Hey! We JUST protected them. Go once more and evaluation them if you could't recite all three.)

The First Cause is that you didn't GE' it in the first place.

The Second Cause is which you didn't CARE sufficient to do something positive about it. You efficiently cope with 2 of the three Causes Of "Forget-ory" really thru taking the time to pay proper interest to someone's name.

Chapter 7: Repetition Is The Mother Of Learning

Repetition is the mother of studying.

Repetition is the mom of analyzing.

Repetition is _____?

Yes... the mom of learning!

You already recognize that whilst you repeat a few component over and over, it has an inclination to stay to your head higher. Isn't that right?

Well then, permit's use what you recognize a manner to do, to enhance your capability to don't forget humans's names.

A clean three Step Method...

If you commonly observe the following three Step Method at the same time as you're assembly human beings for the primary time, you may dramatically decorate your functionality to endure in thoughts their names.

Step 1. Use the call at the same time as you first meet.

Step 2. Use the decision within the route of your intitial communication.

Step 3. Use the call even as you're parting.

Here's an example of ways our friend Joe may use the 3 steps...

Joe:"Hi, I'm Joe. What's your name?"

Mary:"Hello, I'm Mary."

Joe: "Nice to meet you Mary. Great birthday celebration huh? (or irrespective of the event is – simplest a chunk 'small talk' between them right right here. Then in a second or two...)

Joe: "By the way Mary, what form of art work do you do?" (She responds and they hold with a chunk greater 'small speak'. Now the two of them are equipped to element...)

Joe:"It grow to be great assembly you, Mary."

By the use of the person's name 3 times, you will greater in reality embed it in your mind. Don't overdo it although. Keep it sounding herbal. You don't need to use their call in every sentence. (Hello Mary, Mary, Mary.)

Three times is really the proper amount. The starting, middle, and prevent of your first conversation.

Remembering their names at the same time as you notice them yet again.

Well, the 3 Step Method will help you get via an afternoon, or a dinner assembly. But, what about whilst you spot that character over again in a few days? It may also high-quality assist you a hint bit if so.

If you didn't join that man or woman's call to some trouble, you in all likelihood acquired't undergo in mind it the following time you meet.

Merely the usage of repetition is pleasant even as you are meeting only some people, however, what in case you're assembly an entire organisation of dad and mom? What then?

In the following phase you may have a study a chain of very powerful imaging techniques. Using the ones techniques will give you the capability to recollect all of us's name for lengthy durations of time and they'll also be a terrific help to you whilst you are meeting companies of people.

IMAGINATION & CONNECTION

In one word, the 'mystery' to growing a tremendous effective reminiscence is IMAGINATION!

Imagination is a lengthened shape of the phrase picture. Your thoughts holds facts in pictures. The more fantastic an photograph is, the an awful lot much less difficult it's far to keep in mind. It's the way your mind is honestly designed to artwork.

Everything created via the use of mankind first existed in someone's creativeness.

We see pictures in our heads after which seem them in the physical international.

We're going to discover ways to take someone's call, that is an intangible, and make an image out of it.

Often, I pay attention human beings ask about 'Association'.

They've heard, or have a look at, that this 'association' stuff is the crucial aspect to having an top notch reminiscence. But, the problem is that word does no longer resonate nicely with people. It's too tough of a idea to understand without issues.

A plenty better word to apply is CONNECTION.

The 2nd important function of your thoughts is that wants to be part of subjects collectively. You'll frequently pay attention little children say, "You imply like…"?

Right!

The mind desires to located matters in to instructions. This is sort of like that, and so forth. It wants to be part of subjects collectively similar to the quantities of a huge jigsaw puzzle.

In order to take a look at a few element new, you thoughts connects it to a few thing which it has already stored there. Most of the time, those connections display up subconsciously, at lightning pace. You are probable not even aware about them.

However, we can take the time to help your mind multiply its energy through making the ones connections very intentionally. We're going to make the ones creative connections on motive.

So here are the 2 steps.

First: you'll learn how to make snap shots out of humans's names.

Second: you may see a way to sign up for those photographs to the people you're assembly.

Later on this ebook we'll be learning a manner to attach clean, and now and again outrageous pictures to sure tendencies of someone's face or body.

To observe information approximately humans, every now and then we'll be part of those photographs to the accomplishments those human beings are identified for engaging in.

PICTURE THAT NAME

The hassle with names is, earlier than the whole lot glance, maximum of them don't appear to have an effects identifiable picture.

Names are intangible. If the call truly remains a collection of sounds, it's far very difficult to your thoughts to store it efficaciously.

However, if we're capable of 'SEE' the photograph of that name in our minds-eye, it will become very easy to your mind to shop it and later preserve in thoughts it, at will.

There are 4 (four) precise techniques that we're able to take a call and turn it into an photo. We'll then join that picture to the man or woman we're meeting.

We're going to discover every of those ways in depth.

You may additionally additionally speedy begin to apprehend which you've been performing some of these items all alongside. In fact, it's likely that none of those four approaches of imaging, or imagining, a name is surely new to you.

In all hazard, you've been doing this due to the fact you have got been a touch infant.

You see, you're going to be re-analyzing a system that you got here for the duration of accidently. This is some aspect that came manifestly to you. But, because you have been doing it 'by means of the use of way of twist of destiny' it in no way really registered on you.

YOUR NAME RINGS A BELLE

The first way is one of the only. Some names have already got a protected image. That is, the call already has a because of this or is part.

Let's see a few examples.

BILL What's a bill? You get them within the mail all the time. You've have been given to pay them. Also, a duck has a BILL.

MIKEWhat's that? A speaker or singer uses one all of the time (a MICrophone).

MATTYou wipe your feet on a welcome MAT. Wrestlers schooling session on one too.

MARKPut a MARK on a sheet of paper with a MARKer pen.

ROSEThis is an smooth one! It's the lovable flower. Other flower/plant names are VIOLET, IRIS, DAISY, LILLY, IVY, HOLLY, and FERN.

PEARLHere's any other smooth one. You may additionally even private a PEARL necklace. Other gem stone names are SAPHIRE, JADE, RUBY and CRYSTAL.

APRILThe calendar presents us a few other quite names moreover: MAY , JUNE, or maybe TUESDAY. So does the time of day: DAWN and EVE.

HONEYHere are some distinctive delicious names: SUGAR, CHERRY, COCO, and CANDY.

JEANIt's quite easy to endure in thoughts a pair of designer JEANs.

Another clothing item name is probably HATTIE.

BELLEYou've already were given this one, don't you? Just recall a church BELL or the Liberty BELL.

By George, I think you're getting it. You are, aren't you?

Of course you are!

How many distinct names can you think of that already have built-in images?

Here are a few additional guys's names...

Art – Bud – Chuck – Drew – Earl – Frank – Lance – Jack – Oscar – Rich – Robin – Rob – Rod – Rocky – Sandy – Stew – Teddy – Victor – Will

Here are a few additional ladies's names...

Brandi – Dot – Faith – Fanny – Ginger – Grace – Hope – Joy – Mercedes – Olive – Penny – Peg – Sue – Sunny – Star – Toy

Last, however not least...

Here are some examples of human beings's LAST names with included pix.

Baker – Black – Carpenter – Canter – Colt – Duke – Fender – Ford – Gold (Goldsmith, Goldberg, Goldstein, and so forth.) – Green – G roves – Hall – Hill – Holliday – Hunt – Kane – Masters – Mudd – Plummer – Pool – Post – Rivers – Roach – Smith –Steele – Stein – Stone – Walker – Washington – White – Winters – Young

A rose through some different name...

If any distant places languages, you could see many, many names which have integrated pics, despite the fact that they may not have an effects identifiable photograph in English.

For instance, right right here are a few Italian names. Rosa is a rose. Stella way celebrity. Russo is crimson. Russomanno is red hands. (As in I caught you crimson-handed?) And Verde is green. (Giuseppe Verdi, the terrific Italian composer's name translated into English is... Joe Green.)

I'm terrific that you will see many more examples of names that already have integrated pictures, in case you truly appearance and pay attention for them.

Chapter 8: You Remind Me Of Someone

The 2nd manner to transform a person's call into an picture is to attach the decision to someone famous, or to someone in my opinion with the

identical call.

In reality, you're probable already the use of this technique now. But, you're possibly best doing it subconsciously.

Isn't it relatively clean to go through in thoughts the call of someone who has the equal name as you? What approximately the identical name as your mother, father, brother, sister, or every other near relative?

Let's say you're assembly a person named Mark for the number one time. If that occurs to be your brother's name, you can issue out that fact.

This is perfectly herbal detail to do. That's what makes it this form of extraordinary method... you are already doing it genuinely. You need to make this method paintings even higher whilst you do it deliberately.

When you grow to be aware about it, you'll meet many people whose names will remind you of someone else with the equal or comparable name. The idea proper here is to count on the person you are assembly now, interacting in some way with the simplest you know. In your creativeness, you can see them shaking fingers, playing sports activities activities, or speakme together.

Yabba Dabba Doo

Let's take a look at some examples of well-known human beings that have without issue identifiable names and the manner you can make a reference to that new man or woman you are simply meeting.

If you meet someone named Fred, you may think him hanging out with Fred Flintstone, the cool active movie man or woman.

Ronald might also moreover make you think of Ronald McDonald, the famous fast food chain's clown spokesperson.

Jack can also join nicely with Jack Nicholson the actor, or a infant's toy, a Jack-In-The-Box., or possibly the father of health spa corporation, Jack LaLanne (perhaps they're doing jumping Jacks?)

Sam should have you ever consider a poster of Uncle Sam. "I need you."

Tony can also have you ever ever take into account Tony The Tiger from the cereal subject. He's Grrrreat!

Frank would possibly make you consider you studied of Frankenstein.

Women's names are simply as easy.

Mae reminds some people of the antique-time movie celebrity Mae West.

Jacqueline is a call smooth to hook up with the overdue Jacqueline Kennedy-Onassis.

Eve makes many bear in mind Adam and Eve and The Garden of Eden.

Marilyn might be connected to the maximum famous Marilyn of all... Monroe.

Or the rocker: Marilyn Manson.

Last names also may be linked consequences like this too.

Mrs. Taylor, ought to have many humans think about Elizabeth Taylor.

Mr. Letterman would possibly make David Letterman, the overdue night time time host spring to thoughts.

Mr. Bennett can also have a tune fan reflect onconsideration on Tony Bennett.

Mr. Jefferson also can make a records buff reflect onconsideration on Thomas Jefferson. While older dad and mom may take into account a take a seat down down-com TV show and think about George Jefferson.

Ms. Davis might possibly have younger movie fans consider Geena Davis, and older ones recollect Bette Davis.

Mr. Hogan should virtually have any fan of wrestling reflect onconsideration on

"The Hulkster", Mr. Hollywood himself.

This approach will be very powerful! Images you are making this manner will be inclined to last for a totally long time if you have made them without a doubt.

RHYME OR REASON

The 1/three way to create pics for names has been used by kids in playgrounds all through the generations.

You've heard them yourselves. Children making amusing of each different with the useful resource of rhyming a playmate's name:

"Baggy, baggy, raggy, Aggie."

"Bob, Bob, a large fat slob."

"June, you're a goon at the moon."

"Fat Matt ate a rat after which sat on a cat."

This is ready as number one a way as there's. Children aren't taught this. They just do it glaringly. Maybe this brings decrease returned some schoolyard memories.

Let's see how we are able to use it to our very personal nicely benefit.

We've clearly met a young guy call Keith and you be conscious he has a stunning smile. Maybe you would likely make the rhyme, "Keith has top notch tooth".

You meet Mrs. Kelly who is pretty heavy. "Kelly with the huge belly" involves mind.

Marty is next. After speakme with him, you observed that he appears to be quite first rate. "Marty is a smarty".

Jill is an older woman who hasn't been maintaining up with matters. "Jill is over the hill."

Use of the rhyming approach is limited handiest through your creativity. Perhaps this section added returned recollections of being teased as a little one. (Or possibly YOU were the most effective doing the teasing.)

We're definitely using a manner that includes us as children pretty truely; one to help you to boom a powerful recall for people's names. The idea is to recapture the imaginitive, amusing, spirit that lives inner of you. Then you'll be able to create rhymes and photos as with out troubles and as fast as you probably did whilst you have got been a infant.

HOLD DA MAYO

The fourth method to create pix from a person's name is to observe that the decision seems like another phrase or phrase.

Sometimes the call without a doubt reminds you of some thing that sounds similar but is not pretty exactly find it irresistible. We're going to replacement this new phrase or word for the character's call to help us do not forget it. We'll call the ones replacement, sound-alike phrases our CODE WORDS.

Some examples:

Beth looks as if bathtub.

Marsha looks as if Martian.

Nicole seems like nickel.

Al looks like ale.

Harry looks as if furry.

Paul appears like pole.

We can try this with almost any call. The examples are by no means ending.

Let's make a piece Code Word list for some commonplace women's names.

Amy — reason; Ann — ant; Beverly — beverage; Doris — doors; Irene — iron; Julie — jewel; Karen — corn; Linda — lint; Marjorie — margarine; Melanie — melon; Rhoda — avenue; Theresa — timber; Tina — tiny; Yolanda — yo yo

Now, permit's do the equal factor for a few not unusual guys's names.

Andrew — android; Barry — berry; Brian — mind; Carl — curl; Dan — dance; Dave — dove; Doug — dog; Eric — a rock; George — gorge; Jeff — chef; Ken — can; Len — lens; Murray — merry; Neil — kneel; Perry — Perrier; Russ — rust; Sid — sit down; Stan — stand

Last names lend themselves specifically nicely to this sound-alike tool. Often, it's the ONLY way to photo the choice. Since the bulk of last names don't appear to have an with out problem identifiable meaning, we are able to supply the call an photo with the aid of being attentive to what it seems like and adapting it to some thing that can be pictured.

Let's attempt it out.

Bannister sounds precisely like a banister on a stairway.

Caldwell sounds just like a cold nicely.

Drucker sounds similar to drunkard.

Everhardt sounds pretty close to ever difficult, or perhaps to every coronary heart. 1st Earl Baldwin of Bewdley sounds some detail like bald one.

Graham, in case you say it with the right pronunciation, looks as if grey ham.

Johnson is John's son; much like Robertson is Robert's son.

Blake looks like block.

Wallace is quite close to wallets.

Zucker sounds nearly like sucker.

We can also additionally need to undergo the whole cellular telephone e-book gambling this recreation.

This technique is specifically beneficial when attempting to recall very ethnic sounding names. As a depend number of fact, it's the ONLY way I can reflect onconsideration on to make an photo out of hard sounding names.

Let's take a look at out a few. I positioned query marks after the 'translated' code word due to the reality that's what the ones names sound want to me. How approximately to you?

Here are some examples. Say them OUT LOUD and also you'll pay interest it.

Ramsarup - rum syrup?

Seepersad - high-quality sad?

Panday - pan day?

Laimansingh - laymen sing?

Kissoon - kiss fast? (I like that one.)

Hanrahan - hammer hand?

Shaughnessey - Shawn no see?

Peluso - pay low so?

Grillo - grill or gorilla?

Franchino - Frankie! NO! or how about this silly one... A little Frank? (no longer a whole sized frank handiest a frank-ino)

Peragine - pair a jeans?

Trublekowski - trouble cow ski?

Romanov- romance off?

Garachkeiv- garage key?

Krayzelberg - a crazy ice berg, a loopy berg?

Buyanovski - buy sufficient skis?

Teuscher - toy proportion?

Castillo - forged metallic?

Suveges - sue Vegas?

Nguyen - new yen? Also cited 'win'

Champaneria - champagne air yeah?

Dignard - den backyard, or dig in outdoor?

Herrera - her errors?

Ishak - his shack?

Mahmoud - my mood?

Oskroba - Ask robot?

Pottzenmeyer - pots in my ear?

Klachkova - grasp cowl?

Nakesone - Knock a Sony?

Agoncillo - I can see you?

Bellefontaine - bell fountain?

Don't be afraid to be stupid. Have some fun with this.

Be as a touch toddler and unleash your creativity with making up your photographs. Just make sure you maintain the code phrase/photograph as close to as viable to the actual sound of the individual's call you are attempting to undergo in mind.

As some distance as my personal final name, DiMaio, try this photograph on for length. Imagine going proper proper into a delicatessen and ordering a sandwich. Realizing you don't want mayonnaise on it you yell to the deli man... "Hey, keep da' mayo."

In the very last severa pages of this direction, you'll see that I've protected lists of code phrases for men's, women's and last names. Review the ones lists until you turn out to be familiar with them. Then, you may be nicely prepared to fast create an image for someone's call even as not having to anticipate up with one in every of your very personal.

I'LL ALWAYS REMEMBER "WHAT'S HIS FACE"

Now that we've IMAGINED the man or woman's name, allow's see the way to CONNECT it to them.

If we be a part of the image to what that person is carrying in recent times, it would help us out for these days, but the next time we met them, they in all likelihood received't be dressed the equal. We want to make the connection to 3 thing that honestly identifies the character we choice to recollect.

The excellent element to do is be a part of the picture we created to the character's FACE. That is what identifies every us exceptional, isn't it our faces. What separates one man or woman's face from another?

Look, REALLY LOOK, at each face you spot and attempt to pick out out one or greater exquisite capabilities.

For example, you absolutely met a person named Russ. Russ has very purple hair. It might be clean to attach his name which seems like "rust" to the reddish coloration of his hair. The subsequent time you observed him, his crimson hair may make you trust you studied of his name.

Next, you meet a woman named Tina. You note that she has very small eyes. The code word for Tina is "tiny". You can see that she has tiny little eyes. When you be aware her once more you will phrase her eyes, and her name will come flashing once more into your thoughts.

The guy reputation subsequent to her is Mr. Hale. You word that he has deep lines in his brow and along of his mouth. Can you pretend that he has been out in a HAIL hurricane and he has plenty of ice crystals caught in the traces of his forehead and subsequent to his mouth. Mr. Hale is the simplest with the hail on his face.

Finally, you meet Mrs. McKinley. She is a pleasing-searching lady who has a mild bump at the bridge of her nostril. You may additionally additionally exaggerate that bump for your creativeness until it's far as big as Mount McKinley. See that photograph on your thoughts now: the bump developing and growing, till it's as big as Mt. McKinley. When you note her all all over again you can bear in thoughts her call.

Let's see how nicely you consider the 4 human beings you truely met.

What become the selection of the person with the pink hair?

That's proper - Russ.

Who become the woman with the tiny eyes?

Very proper! - Tina.

How about the person with the deep traces in his face?

Right all over again. - Mr. Hale.

The girl with the bump on her nostril changed into...?

Yes. - Mrs. McKinley.

You see, you're getting the hang of it already!

If you neglected any of the names of these people, it's miles most effective due to the fact you didn't make a easy sufficient photo to your thoughts's eye. Don't permit that discourage you. Remember, that may be a modern day idea for you. Give it a risk to SINK IN.

In the ebook you'll see I've protected a chart of facial developments that will help you out. Next, we can speak a number of the ones traits to motive them to much less hard in case you need to perceive.

Chapter 9: Chart Of Facial Characteristics

IS HE A SQUARE OR WHAT?

In this phase, we'll use actors and actresses who must in all likelihood be identified thru those of you to your 50's and older. This is to provide you unique examples of people whose faces have the specific developments I'm describing.

For those of you younger parents analyzing this, you could not right away apprehend some of the ones celebrities. That's OK. We'll also use some cutting-edge examples.

It's quite smooth to discover pictures at the net of all the examples mentioned proper here so that you can see their faces for your self.

You also can begin thinking of human beings you can in my opinion recognize who've similar facial trends to the examples we're the use of right here.

Notice the SHAPE of someone's face.

Some human beings have very spherical faces. Dom DeLuise is a extraordinary instance of a person who has a round face. Some contemporary examples is probably singer Kelly Clarkson and actress Kirsten Dunst.

Someone with a square face is Jacqueline Kennedy Onassis. In your mind eye, picture her for a 2d. Can you spot her square jaw? Angelina Jolie is probably an super instance of another actress with a squarish commonplace face.

Victoria Principal is a great instance of someone who has a coronary coronary heart-customary or triangular face. It is extensive on the top and she or he or he has a small chin. Leonardo DiCaprio and Scarlett Johansson are some suitable present day-day-day examples.

For an oval face Meryl Streep entails thoughts. Some different nicely examples are Jada Pinkett Smith and Beyonce' Knowles.

Celebrities with slim faces might also embody comedian actors Dick Van Dyke and Stan Laurel of Laurel and Hardy. Liv Tyler and Kim Kardashian every have slender faces.

IT'S GETTING HAIRY

Another feature this is apparent is the hair.

Notice how unique some human beings's hair may be. You might also moreover furthermore meet someone with very blond or even white hair, like Andy Wharhol.

You would possibly notice someone who had exquisite red hair like Lucille Ball. The salt-and-pepper appearance might also remind you of a person great searching— Omar Shariff, in all likelihood.

Notice how a wonderful deal hair a person has. You can also see someone with a lovable whole head of hair, someone whose hairline is receding, or each other who is balding.

Notice too, the STYLE of the hair. Is it very right away, wavy, wildly curly, or is it frizzy?

Look at facial hair. Does he have sideburns? How about a beard? Is it complete or smartly trimmed? Does he have a mustache? What does it look like? Bushy? Long? Down-grew to turn out to be? Does SHE have a mustache?

How about eyebrows? Are they hairy? ...plucked? ...or painted on?

Are they set enormous apart or are they connected together as one massive eyebrow?

Some people have 'well-known' hair:

Don King

James Brown

Al Sharpton

Donald Trump

Others have had iconic facial hair.

Groucho Marx

Charlie Chaplin

Tom Sellek

Elvis had his sideburns

and allow's no longer forget about approximately ZZ Top

On a personal be aware, I purposely keep my very own mustache trimmed in a first rate manner and a few component that permits people to do not forget my face lots much less complex.

THE EYES HAVE IT

Pay particular interest to someone's eyes.

In truth, even as taking stock of a person's facial traits make it a addiction to have a take a look at the colour and shape of a person's eyes first. Doing that will help you set up on a not unusual starting point with the face of sincerely everyone you meet.

Color is the number one detail to search for. Some people have been famous for his or her toddler blues Paul Newman, as an instance. One of Frank Sinatra's many nicknames grow to be 'Ole Blue Eyes.

There are those who will marvel you with how dark their eyes are.

Others have flecks of gold within the iris. Others have eyes which is probably very light.

Notice the scale of the eyes. Are the eyes massive or are they little and beady? What shape are they? ...round, almond, slanted?

Does the person you're assembly have circles beneath their eyes or deep crow's ft inside the corners? Look for what makes them identifiable.

If you are making your first actual mission to reputation on someone's eyes on the same time as you meet them, you'll have established the right attitude to analyze their specific facial trends.

LEND ME YOUR EARS

Look at every person's ears.

Some humans have ears that flare faraway from the pinnacle.

The 1930's main guy, Clark Gable had ears like that.

I've take a look at that Barak Obama is touchy approximately his ears.

Prince Charles has some famous ears.

Harrison Ford and Will Smith have massive ears.

Some human beings have little tiny ears.

Some are missing a part of an ear. Stephen Colbert is lacking a part of his right ear due to a tumor while he turn out to be a toddler.

A character who became a boxer or wrestler might probably have a cauliflower ear.

The combined martial artist Randy Coutoure has ears like that.

Sometimes you'll see some older guys which have hair developing out in their ears. I knew a person as quickly as I lived in Trinidad who had so much ear hair that it seemed like a bush growing out of his ears.

How about jewelry? Are the ears pierced? How often? These days it's far elegant for women to have many earrings in on ear.

Some men have pierced ears. Notice them.

What approximately ear lobes? Some are large and placing. Some are slightly there.

THE NOSE KNOWS

The nose every so often desires no exaggeration.

You will see an limitless form of noses.

Many human beings have emerge as well-known for them.

Here are a number of them

Jimmy Durante

Jamie Farr (Klinger on Mash)

Danny Thomas

All three of those well-known humorous guys had huge noses.

Karl Malden

Barbara Streisand

Owen Wilson

Each of them have uniquely formed noses.

Bob Hope modified into famous for his upturned 'ski-slope' nose.

Some have best little noses. Others have hawk-like talents.

Is it pug, bent, crooked, flat, huge, narrow, upturned, or is it perfectly

right away?

MORE CHINS THAN A CHINESE PHONEBOOK

A individual's chin may be an extremely good identifying feature too.

Many film stars have chins which may be with out trouble remembered.

Kirk Douglas had a round dimple in his.

Some well-known actors with cleft chins embody

John Travolta

Ben Affleck

Aaron Eckhart

Matt Damon

Cary Grant

James Garner

One of the actors from the TV Show Burn Notice, Bruce Campbell, has this form of notable chin that jokes approximately it were frequently made in severa episodes.

Perhaps no chin is more well-known than the best belonging to Jay Leno.

Some humans have big chins. Some are so small they not regularly have a chin in any respect. Heavy people might also additionally have double chins.

YOU THINK SHE'S GOT A BIG MOUTH

Look at a person's mouth.

You will see humans with small pursed lips. Some humans have nearly no lips in any respect, while others may also moreover have complete or perhaps thick lips.

Some humans have very huge, massive mouths. Joe E. Brown have become well-known for his in his films of the 1940's.

People who've a one among a kind mouth and/or lips:

Julia Roberts

Angelina Jolie

Ray Charles

Phyliss Diller

Gary Shandling

Joaquin Phoenix

Stacy Keach

One of the maximum well-known mouths of all time belongs to Rolling Stone

Mick Jagger

Notice people's enamel. Do they've straight away, even teeth ; pearly, white enamel;

tooth with gaps among them; crooked teeth; or are they wearing braces?

Some well-known hole toothed smiles belong to:

Michael Strahan

Brigette Bardot

Lauren Hutton

Natalie Cole

And of route... David Letterman

DON'T STARE

All those facial developments combine to make up one precise face.

There aren't any faces perfectly alike. Even the mothers of identical twins are capable to tell them apart... most of the time.

It is as lots as you to select one or facial inclinations that will help you turn out to be aware of the character you are assembly.

When you check them on the equal time as being introduced, be observant. You don't have to be apparent about it and stare. You don't need to mention, "Hey, ought to you switch a bit sideways for me, I want to get a better have a have a have a look at your ears."

Chapter 10: Putting It All Together

Now that we've located out to make photographs for people's names and furthermore have a take a look at their facial tendencies, permit's see the manner to positioned all of them collectively.

We are going to meet a few people collectively

As I introduce every of them to you, I would like you to create pictures for his or her names and be a part of the ones photographs to their faces.

The first man or woman we'll meet is called Mr. Archie Jackson. We can see that Mr. Jackson has an Afro hair fashion. He has a few strains in his forehead, and he has massive, bushy eyebrows. His first name, Archie, seems like "arch." In your creativeness you could see the strains in his brow usual like massive arches. For your picture of arches you may see the Golden Arches of MacDonald's, or the Arch of

Triumph in Paris. Put an arch within the traces of his forehead. Also placed some arches in his Afro. See them coming right up via his hair. See that stupid image now. For an photograph of his final call, Jackson, you may probable see a vehicle's bumper jack. Imagine bumper jacks protecting up his huge, heavy, bushy eyebrows. They are so heavy, they need the jacks to preserve them up. Arches on his brow and in his hair, jacks below his eyebrows... Archie Jackson.

The subsequent person we're able to meet is Linda Polanski. Linda has stunning lengthy blond hair and a lovely upturned little nostril. The code phrase for Linda is "lint." See masses of lint in her cute hair. See lots of portions of fuzz, hundreds of lint in that hair. See it. Her final call, Polanski, appears like "pole and ski." Think of a ski pole. Now notice her nose. She's have been given such a ski slope form of noses. Pretend a person is skiing down her nose and protective ski poles. See those ski poles on her nose. Lint in her hair, ski pole on her nose... will become Linda Polanski.

The 0.33 person we are delivered to is Mr. Al O'Brien. Al impresses you as a completely sensible man. You'll right now be conscious that he has a very thick, furry beard and mustache. The name Al looks like "ale." You might also see him drinking ale and spilling it into his beard. His beard is sopping wet with ale. His remaining name, O'Brien seems like "a thoughts." He can be very smart. He is a actual mind. Ale is his beard, very clever: "ale a thoughts" turns into...Al O'Brien.

Marjorie LeBeau is the following one we'll meet. Marjorie is an older lady with massive jowls and greying hair. You be aware that her eyeglasses seem to preserve sliding down her nostril, too. The name Marjorie appears like "margarine." Pretend that her glasses keep sliding because of the reality she has margarine on her nostril. Perhaps you may stuff her cheeks with margarine

129

simply so her jowls puff out, too. Her ultimate name, LeBeau, sounds like "a bow." Put pretty, brightly coloured bows in her greying hair. See them sincerely. Margarine and bows will remind you of Marjorie LeBeau.

Next, we are brought to Carmine Gallo. Carmine, you'll note proper away, has a whole head of thick, curly hair and a huge jaw. He also has a nose this is slightly bent. Carmine's first call starts offevolved offevolved with the word "automobile." You might imagine a car crashing into his nose, and that's the manner it were given bent. By the manner, whose vehicle is it? The automobile is mine ...car-mine. His last name, Gallo, may additionally remind you of Gallo wines, that could be a well-known logo call. You could in all likelihood see your self pouring Gallo wine at some stage in his thick curly hair. Of course, we only IMAGINE that we attempt this to Carmine.

The 6th character we're going to fulfill has an uncommon sounding name. She is from the Orient, and her name is Hahn Orhyu. When meeting Hahn, we also can have some problem at the begin because her call is so unique. By the usage of the strategies we've got determined out up to now, we will be capable of master her call without problems as properly. Her first call, Hahn, may additionally additionally make you take delivery of as genuine with you studied of Heinz ketchup. You take a look at that her hair is jet black and immediately. Pour some Heinz in her hair. See it dripping down, thick and red. Her very last name, Orhyu , looks like "Oreo," Oreo cookies. Notice her nose and the little traces along her nostril. Put the Oreo cookies on her nostril and inside the ones little lines. "Heinz Oreo" will become Hahn Orhyu.

MINI QUIZ

Now, permit's see how you're doing to this point. We'll have a hint quiz.

What is the first call of the lady with the prolonged blond hair?

Remember we positioned lint in it? Yes, her name is Linda. How approximately her ultimate call? Imagine her nostril. What did we positioned there? Right...ski pole...Polanski. Very proper!

What is the choice of the character with the traces in his brow, the Afro, and the heavy eyebrows? What did you notice in his hair and brow? What have become maintaining up the ones heavy eyebrows? O.K. Now, what's his name? Did you are pronouncing Archie Jackson? Good for you!

What approximately the older female with the gray hair whose glasses stored sliding? What brought on them to slide? That's right, the margarine. Her first call is Marjorie. In her gray hair you located a few component-- bows. Right, her final call is LeBeau.

The clever gentleman with the complete beard is who? What did he spill in his beard? Ale. He is sensible, a real mind. What is his call? Correct…Al O'Brien!

What is the name of the person with the bent nostril, massive jaw, and curly hair? You observed the auto crashing into his nostril bending it, and the wine in his hair. His call is…Carmine Gallo. Right!

Lastly we've the lady from the Orient. Remember the ketch-up and the cookies? What is her name? If you said Hahn Orhyu, you are right again!

How did you do on this quiz? Pretty true, I'll guess. If you obtain six out of six accurate, you have already got an extremely good hold close to of the concept. If you disregarded any, it's far high-quality due to the reality the pictures on your thoughts have been now not made really enough. Sometimes, because I am making the photographs for you at this issue, you may now not see them as truely as if you were making them for yourself.

HOW TO MEET GROUPS OF PEOPLE

Frequently, a person will visit a assembly or to a party and upon arriving, the boss or the host will make the introductions with the useful resource of damn off an entire collection of names: "Joe, that is BillBobPeteMaryJeanJohnFredFrankCarlaandLaura.I'd which includes you all to satisfy Joe." Of course, it's very difficult to get the names like that, so for the rest of the time people name each exclusive, "pal," "buddy," "honey," "highly-priced" and so forth. How do you manage this commonplace state of affairs?

One way of coping with this incidence is to ARRIVE EARLY to the meeting or birthday celebration. This way, you're assembly pleasant one or humans at a time, as an possibility of having to meet a whole institution. This will come up with the time you need to meet anybody at a time. By the time topics get going, you'll recognize pretty masses everyone inside the room. It will provide you with a outstanding feeling of self notion.

If you're added to a collection of humans , start a communication with one in each of them and say some thing to the impact, "I emerge as delivered to you so rapid that I didn't get your call." People may be flattered which you take an hobby in who they may be. As subjects improvement, do the identical detail with actually everyone you were added to that you want to fulfill nicely. Don't ever be afraid to invite someone yet again, "What's your name?" People in reality DO need to be remembered.

After meeting some human beings, get off to the element of the room for a 2nd and make your highbrow snap shots for their names. Do it with surely all of us you truly met. Create the image for their name and be part of it to them in a few way. Then circulate and meet some extra people and repeat the equal system. Don't try to do it with a set of twenty or thirty people abruptly, because of the fact you'll possibly get careworn and discouraged. Work with small organizations of human beings at a time. Get off to the side, make your images, after which skip meet a few greater.

LOVERS AND OTHER STRANGERS

Let's learn how to consider the names of couples, their kids, and every different individual they are with. When you meet one-half of of of that couple again you'll also remember the accomplice. This could make humans enjoy that you are being involved and considerate. Remembering the call of a accomplice, baby, or distinct specific person will make a totally favorable effect.

The first couple you'll be delivered to is Al and his associate Terry. Al, who we met in advance, has a complete beard. His partner Terry has thick, curly hair. The code word for Al we already realise is "ale." See Al having ale spilled into his beard, making it sopping moist. The code word for Terry is "terrycloth." You could probable see strips of terrycloth tied into curly hair. Now, allow's mentally be part of Al and his spouse, Terry. The ALE gets spilled and he wishes a TERRY material to wipe it up. Now, we've been able to be a part of the two of their names together. When you spot Al once more, you would possibly ask how his wife Terry is.

The next couple is Frank and his partner Nicole. Frank has a neatly trimmed mustache and Nicole has stunning, massive, darkish eyes. The code phrase for Frank is "frankfurter." You may also additionally need to see a frankfurter on his lip in preference to that trim mustache. The code word for Nicole is "nickel." You may additionally see yourself putting nickels on her huge eyes. To join them collectively you could image biting proper right into a frankfurter and locating out it turned into truly a roll of nickels. Feel those nickels clinging round in opposition in your teeth. When you determined of Frank, the image of nickels (Nicole) may additionally additionally come lower decrease back to you.

Now you are delivered to Art and Roxanne. Art, who has a massive, rectangular-formed face, may make you think of him having a square image body round his face, like a chunk of art. Roxanne is rather heavy, making you watched that possibly she would probably have rocks (Rocks anne) in her get dressed. To be a part of the names together, you notice yourself taking the rocks and throwing them through a portray, via the paintings. When you meet her once more, that stupid image will remind you of his call, too.

Lastly, you meet Keith and Donna and their youngsters, Karen and Mark. Keith has massive flaring ears. Perhaps we might also want to hold keys, which seems like "Keith," from his large ears like earrings. Donna has a mole on her cheek. "Donut" is the code word for Donna. You can also see that she has a donut on her cheek wherein that mole is. Their daughter Karen has beautiful, even, white teeth. "Karen" looks as if "corn." You could probably placed yellow corn in amongst her tooth. Or supply her quantities of corn in choice to teeth. Now accept as true with her smiling with the corn there. Mark is the toddler and he has jet black hair. For your image of his name you can faux to colour his hair black with a Magic MARKer.

Let's keep in mind the names of the mother and father and their children all collectively. To try this we'll make a list of the code phrases: keys, donut, corn, and marker. See these silly images. Take a key and stick it into the hole of the donut to unlock it. Next, take the donut and slip an ear of corn through the hollow. Then shade the kernels of the corn black with a marker. Now see that complete list of photos in your mind. The key unlocks the donut. The donut has a corn slipped thru the hole. Color the corn with the marker. What we've were given got accomplished is create a chain of pix associated collectively. You will examine extra approximately this idea inside the software on remembering lists.

ANOTHER LITTLE QUIZ

Now, permit's see how your reminiscence is doing to this point. What is the call of the person with the heavy complete beard? Right...Al. His beard is sopping moist from the ale. His spouse has thick, curly hair. What did we tie into her hair? Right over again... Terrycloth. Her name is Terry.

Who is the accomplice of the person with the trimmed mustache? Ask your self his name first. What did you put on his lip? The FRANKfurter...then you definately bit into it and what modified into clanging around on your mouth? That's proper, nickels. Nicole is her call. She turn out to be the handiest with massive eyes that we located the nickels on.

Who is Roxanne's husband? You threw the rocks on the Art. That's right, Art!

The guy with the flaring ears—name is what? You placed the keys at the eats...Keith. What is his spouse's call? What did you free up with the key? Donut, Donna. Good!

The names in their kids are...Karen and...Mark. Right. You slipped the corn thru the donut and painted the kernels of the corn with the marker.

Chapter 11: Long-Term Memory Of Names

Remembering people's names in the way I've defined so far is fantastic at the same time as you attend a party and also you want to get each person's call. By the usage of those strategies you will be capable of undergo in thoughts their names for some days in some time. But approximately more than one weeks or a month or two later—will you still keep in mind the names? Not in case you don't do some thing similarly to what you've accomplished up to now.

If you're clearly interested by being capable of preserve in thoughts human beings's names for a long term, it's far important which you meet them time and again yet again. Since that's no longer constantly possible in actual lifestyles, I'm going to speak approximately a manner that you can try this via use of your creativeness.

As you already know from experience, REPETITION IS THE MOTHER OF LEARNING.

Information that is repeated over and over yet again can be saved thru the mind higher and additional absolutely. If you notable offer your self ONE publicity to records you need to endure in mind, you're substantially handicapping yourself.

To recall the names of the human beings you meet, on the equal time as a long term goes with the aid of in advance than seeing them yet again, it is essential that allows you to use the following device. At the end of your day, make a listing of the new humans you have got met. Write down their names, the facial or physical dispositions you positioned, and every different facts approximately them, in order that a smooth photograph of them will although exist for your thoughts. Review this list of names and statistics in three or 4 days, and recollect what everyone seemed like as you do that. Repeat this system over again in in step with week and another time in a month. This manner it's miles as in case you are seeing them over again. You'll offer your thoughts its wished repetitions to hold the ones people glowing to your mind.

By keeping unique facts of who you meet, you could offer your self a effective gain. Let's say you're a baby-kisser or a salesperson and you are to deal with a set of humans that you met simplest as soon as months in the past, If you walk into the room and are able to name anybody you formerly met thru name after no longer having seen them for several months, you could in truth have them in your facet. You will benefit an lousy lot assist from people whilst you display such notable interest in them. It is manifestly really properly well worth the small amount of attempt it takes to hold unique facts and to check them sometimes.

REMEMBERING FACTS ABOUT PEOPLE

How can we use what we've decided out to date to assist us keep in thoughts records about people? The first step in remembering statistics about humans is to take all people reality and make an picture for it. Then, what we'll do is be part of the photographs to the name.

We're going to make a few innovative connections about famous people that we've observe approximately in our history books and within the newspaper. You should use the identical concept to keep in thoughts subjects about human beings you meet in your each day lifestyles, additionally.

If I asked you to call the number one man to set foot on the moon, would possibly you proper away are aware about it became Neil Armstrong? How can we take into account that Neil Armstrong became the primary guy on the moon? Let's IMAGE his name. He flapped his STRONG ARMS (Armstrong) and flew to the moon. When he have been given there he modified into so tired that he had to KNEEL (Neil) down. Neil Armstrong, first guy at the moon.

Another man or woman well-known from our statistics books is Madame Curie. She come to be the number one person to discover radium and she or he or he experimented with radioactivity. Her final name, Curie, appears like "remedy." Radioactivity can be imaged as radio. She needed to CURE her unwell RADIO. It's a stupid picture, but smooth to make the connection.

Who have end up the primary American girl in outer location? It have emerge as Sally Ride. She turned into the number one girl to RIDE in outer location for the Americans.

What is the decision of the quarterback who took the Miami Dolphins to the Superbowl in 1985? His name is Dan Marino. His last call, Marino, seems like "marina." Where ought to you discover dolphins? Of direction... inside the marina. After he rankings a landing, have you ever visible a football participant dance spherical in the long run vicinity? Sure. "Dan" looks as if "dance." The DANcing football participant inside the MARINA with the dolphins... Dan Marino.

Back in 1986 the top of Japan changed into Prime Minister Nakesone. Perhaps you observed that may be a tough name to consider, however it's miles without a doubt very easy. There is a famous Japanese electronics industrial enterprise agency named Sony. I'm nice you've heard of it. If you go to Japan, you need to never KNOCK A SONY. Nakesone... Prime Minister of Japan.

Also once more in 1986 the selection of the Prime Minister of West Germany end up Helmut Kohl. "Helmut" appears like "helmet." What form of helmet? Think of the WW11 German army helmet with its remarkable shape. Was the helmet warmth? No, it became COLD, (Kohl). Maybe you

147

could see it being complete of COAL. Head of West Germany... Helmut Kohl.

Margaret Mead, the well-known anthropologist, is cited for her have a examine of human beings in an extended way flung lands, particularly Samoa. Her final name, Mead, sounds like "meet." "Samoa" seems like a slur of the phrases "some more." We can say Margaret favored to "Mead Samoa human beings" (meet some greater humans).

The lady credited with the concept of the usage of Seeing-Eye puppies to help the blind have emerge as Mrs. Eustice.

"G.O. C.C.R."

By manner of evaluation, permit's cover the 5 steps needed to keep in mind people's names. Follow these steps in order and soon you'll a maze others collectively with your reminiscence electricity. Even more importantly, you could amaze yourself.

Here are the FIVE STEPS to remembering names:

STEP 1: GET THE NAME RIGHT AND USE IT THREE TIMES.

STEP 2: OBSERVE FACIAL AND BODILY CHARACTERISTICS.

STEP three: CREATE AN IMAGE FOR THE NAME.

STEP 4: CONNECT THE IMAGE OF THE NAME TO THE PERSON.

STEP 5: REVIEW THE NAMES AND CONNECTIONS PERIODICALLY.

You can bear in mind those 5 steps, in order, with using the approach I call "ALPHABET SOUP." We'll use the initials of the primary word in each step: Get, Observe, Create, Connect, Review.

I am keen on a band which have end up famous inside the past due 60's: Creedence

Clearwater Revival. They went via the initials C.C.R.

AN EASY WAY TO PRACTICE

The techniques you have got were given had been given determined out on this software program will offer you with extraordinary memory strength once you get acquainted with them.

It is vital that you workout the ones techniques every chance you get.

As , REPETITION IS THE MOTHER OF LEARNING.

One way to exercise resultseasily is whilst you watch TV. As characters are brought within the films and suggests you're looking, use what you've placed right here to take into account their names. Get their names, have a have a look at what they appear like, create an picture for his or her call, and be part of it to them.

This will offer you with a pressure-free way to apply what you've learned, because handiest you could understand in case you neglect a name or in case you don't forget it. No one's emotions will get damage in case you overlook a name here and there.

You can also use this idea when you are reading the newspaper or a mag and also you stumble upon a photograph. Use "G.O. C.C.R." and see your abilties amplify in a take into account of days. The great factor about it's far that it'll provide you with TREMENDOUS CONFIDENCE to your new energy.

PRACTICE MAKES PERMANENT

Just like some different expertise, it takes a while to turn out to be gifted at remembering humans's names.

Don't grow to be discouraged if you aren't a draw near of these strategies after analyzing or taking note of this facts simplest as quickly as.

Use the concept of SPACED REPETITION to allow your thoughts to digest and assimilate this records over a duration of at the least six repetitions. Each new time you evaluation this fabric, you'll recognize it higher, and it becomes a herbal a part of you.

WILL ALL THIS MAKE YOU PERFECT?

By making use of what you've found out in this software program, you can surpass your antique standard performance by using manner of way of extremely good leaps!

But does this advocate that you'll in no manner ever neglect a call once more?

If you need to apprehend if you could achieve perfection, my solution is NO.

No human will ever be PERFECT at something.

The idea is to end up as real as you may, to stay up on your fantastic capability. Even although you can from time to time slip up, you could though be higher than absolutely everyone else you recognize.

The huge blessings that watch for you, with the aid of manner of remembering human beings's names, are clearly properly worth the effort to research and exercise the strategies furnished right proper here.

With your new-located abilities to bear in mind people's names, you'll benefit first-rate self-self assurance. You can become extra famous. You will earn the honour and admiration of all you are to be had in contact with. You'll accumulate extra achievement, socially further to professionally.

Chapter 12: If You Could Only Do One Thing

People need solutions as brief as viable, however with memorizing names, there can be simplest a lot that you can do proper away.

Sound self-explanatory? Not so speedy. During college, I made my dwelling by the usage of performing close to-up magic at private events. I must walk in with a deck of playing cards and try to carry out for each vacationer on the birthday party as they socialized. Around the same time, I met a polymath and expert magician named Jason Randal, who graciously commenced out to mentor me. During honestly one in every of our many discussions, Jason asked me why people have me at their sports.

"To idiot their web page traffic?"

Nope!

"To do card hints?"

Wrong again.

We went down this course for some time until he eventually gave me the solution. My pastime as an entertainer turned into to alternate the way that humans enjoy, and magic have come to be handiest the automobile. He advised me that most magicians show up with the cause to fool their audiences, and this is precisely what they do. But it definitely is ALL they do.

He taught me that if I confirmed up with the purpose to be an envoy of goodwill, to certainly AFFECT the guests in a high nice way, I can also want to nevertheless supply at the fooling detail even as bringing an lousy lot extra to the table. If I endeavored to make a real reference to each traveller even as a laugh them, I want to really redesign their night. Conversely, if I did no longer display up proceeding to make a real connection, I possibly may want to no longer. As Andrea Bocelli stated, "All that counts in lifestyles is purpose."

Much like raising the temper at celebration, memorizing names requires that you have the proper INTENT. Showing up at a party and letting the names pass in a unmarried ear and out the other is similar to walking onto a baseball area without a glove. You've out of place the struggle earlier than beginning the battle. Without intending to memorize names, you are now not possibly to perform that.

When you move for a jog, what is the primary trouble you do? You probable placed on exercise clothes and walking shoes. When people struggle to workout, behavioral psychologists have positioned that it makes a massive difference at the same time as people lay out workout garments near their beds. When any character wakes up and receives dressed to education consultation, they're more likely to take a look at through. Their clothes offer them a cause. They have primed their brains and eliminated a barrier to get admission to.

So subsequent time you visit an event, add a small reminder to your calendar that a part of your motive that nighttime can be to keep in mind names. If you show up with out the proper purpose, you are leaving it to risk that you may be a hit. You may additionally take into account the names of humans you meet, in any other case you could not. If you show up intending to preserve in thoughts more names than you'll generally, you can at least be more likely to be successful.

Of path, to without a doubt make use of the competencies in this e-book, you may want a bit more than just purpose. You'll additionally need to workout. These abilties are just like studying an tool, the manner to adventure a bicycle, or a way to type. There is an earlier try this is required, but once the capabilities set is mastered, it's miles something that you could hold onto forever.

Chapter 13: A Primer On Memory

As a little one, I loved The Neverending Story films. In The Neverending Story 2, the villain creates a device that strips humans of their reminiscences, which are represented as singular crystal balls. This is how most human beings recall our recollections. We take into account that when we remember a few aspect, the whole memory is pulled as an entire from an internal catalog to the main edge of our brain. While this seems logical, it could not be similarly from the truth.

Recalling activities from our beyond is based on what is referred to as episodic reminiscence (memories approximately unique moments). This isn't like semantic memory (used for random facts and history) and procedural memory (a manner to do topics, just like the use of a motorcycle). Each time we consider some thing, we collect the tale from severa additives of our brains, and small errors creep in.

Over enough retellings of the tale, remarkable factors stay and sure elements depart, and what we're left with will become encoded. These "information" emerge as the memories we tell, despite the fact that the recollections are often incorrect. If you have got ever stumbled upon an vintage magazine, you can have professional searching once more on a reminiscence and since what truly took place is a long way tremendous than what you have recalled. It's the identical motive that eyewitness testimony is so problematic. Humans are obviously horrible at retaining highbrow statistics. That's why we depend lots on the written phrase.

Our operating reminiscence (quick-time period reminiscence) can only hold approximately seven portions of statistics at a time, and the fashionable studies suggests that some factor above six quantities is a stretch for maximum. How do we conquer this and end up superhuman at memorizing names?

The desired precept entails the use of a mnemonic aid. Think of a mnemonic as a bit of data that acts as a bridge to some thing else. Every time we encode a memory, we essentially region a ebook randomly on a library shelf. We want a manner to find out the ebook later if we want to take a look at it once more. If you recollect the Dewey Decimal System, you could recognize that it's miles a category tool created via libraries to discover any ebook at the shelf. When I even have emerge as a toddler, I have to constantly head to section 793.Eight for the magic books. If you aren't a magician, that variety approach no longer something to you. You want context.

Items lacking context are notoriously tough to hold in thoughts, and you're stuck excellent together together with your rote reminiscence (memory through repetition), which can be the manner you remembered everything in simple school. This e-book is all about bypassing your rote reminiscence even as walking with names.

We create the ones mnemonic bridges through affiliation. If you meet all of us named Rob, you may without delay create a intellectual image tying them via a few technique to "rob" ... Maybe they'll be robbing a financial group? Maybe they robbed you of your pockets? By growing this photo, you boom your hazard of later recalling that name.

Now you may be wondering to your self, "Why should I need to characteristic a step as soon as I'm already suffering to remember names?" If you mirror on the names which you keep in mind without issues, you could realise that you already do that. Imagine that you have a brother named Austin. Your first belief whilst you meet a few different Austin is, "That can be clean to bear in thoughts. He stocks my brother's name!" Your brother is now the bridge, and on the equal time as you see that character, you're able to link them to some factor smooth to do not forget (your brother), as opposed to an intangible piece of facts.

This entire e book is ready enhancing topics which you already do and coaching you the manner to create those bridges more successfully. Memorizing names comes down to 3 simple steps, which I name The 3Cs, and after running in the path of the device for just a piece of time, you may find that it starts offevolved to appear in reality. Even if it feels a bit bizarre at the begin, it truely is ok! Increasing your reminiscence via manner of way of even twenty percentage is a first-rate start, and as an advantage, you may be unlocking some of your herbal creativity at the equal time.

Chapter 14: The System The 3cs

The tool for remembering names isn't very complex. You'll do the perfect equal 3 matters, within the actual identical order, each and on every occasion. It's as easy as "The 3Cs."

C1. Create a CARICATURE

C2. Choose a CODE Word

C3. CHANGE the Person

That's it in a nutshell. It is not specifically tough, and I'll provide an reason behind the naked bones within the next few pages in advance than we dive in deeper. For now, allow's begin with a particular example. Look on the photo underneath and take into account that this man or woman is called Adam.

When you examine Adam, what do you notice first?

Most humans have a propensity to have a facial feature this is memorable or effects recognizable. Think of this as what an artist would possibly accentuate in a CARICATURE or cool animated film of the character. In Adam's case, I have to notice his beard, in particular thinking about it is so lengthy and suggested.

The first element we do is take a look at the beard and pick out it due to the fact the outstanding characteristic. Now that we have were given executed that, we get to select a CODE WORD, that is the bridge we use to get us to Adam. My code phrase for every Adam I meet is "apple." You can reflect onconsideration on Adam and Eve and the apple from the Garden of Eden, or extra in fact, of an "Adam's Apple."

Now you need to CHANGE them one manner or the other via affecting them along aspect your code phrase. In this example, we are pretending that his beard hangs so low due to the variety of apples hiding internal of it. Or perhaps he works for Apple secretly! Our new photo of Adam might be something like this:

How is this beneficial? Well, while we see Adam next, we are able to see his beard, so you can purpose the photograph we made with the apples, and the apples will lead us proper lower once more to the call Adam. Every time we meet an Adam, we're able to choose a CARICATURE feature, pick out the CODE WORD apple, and CHANGE that function with the apples in some way.

Why does this paintings so well? We keep in mind images an extended manner better than phrases. Psychologists call this the picture superiority effect. This is why savvy entrepreneurs gift fancy infographics in preference to virtually explaining their product. We keep in mind the images higher than any terms they will present to us. Even in novels, the great authors artwork difficult to use illustrative language in order that we create photographs in our mind's eye.

Essentially, using The 3Cs forces us to transform statistics from some thing intangible (a name) to some thing that we're capable of visualize.

Any tool is handiest as specific as its weakest link, and there are number one locations wherein I see people struggle when mastering to hold in thoughts names. The first includes no longer knowledge the code terms internal and out, that could be a few difficulty we're in a position to talk at duration. The second is simply that many human beings in no way take the time to use the device.

Most mother and father show up at an event or a assembly with one million specific matters on our minds. "Did I located on the right difficulty?" "What will the companions at the business employer don't forget me?" "Will they choose my pitch?" The closing trouble on our minds is remembering people's names, and as a end result they go in one ear and out the other.

Next time you step out to a dinner with new buddies, to a networking occasion, or to meet the cutting-edge day hires, it is essential that you create the proper mind-set and tell yourself which you WILL don't forget anybody's call which you meet. This is plenty less approximately self-affirmation and in addition about priming yourself with the right cause.

Set a smooth motive for the midnight, keeping in mind that this aim will evolve as you get more snug with the strategies. If you goal to keep in mind the call of surely all of us inside the room in your first attempt, you can get bad consequences and surrender. But in case you handiest try and recollect three to four new names, you'll benefit the self guarantee to memorize more at the following skip-round. We get better on the matters we paintings at, easy and easy. So it should not come as a surprise to you that you will need to do subjects a piece differently.

The first detail that you may do is supply yourself every opportunity to get earlier. Back inside the Nineties, a records reporter have become interviewing Siegfried & Roy, at the time the top notch-paid and most-lauded magicians in the international. When the reporter asked how the two met, Roy checked out Siegfried and laughed, announcing, "Siegfried, apparently they haven't finished their homework!" That question were asked in such some of interviews that the duo didn't feel adore it merited their time. Talk show hosts and journalists excel at their jobs thru learning their interviewees and finding the right questions to provide compelling interviews. They do their homework.

At your subsequent occasion, make sure to do YOUR homework. If you attend a marriage, appearance over the names of the human beings sitting at your desk and take a second to make your self acquainted. If you have got were given already memorized the code phrases for the names, anticipate them thru for a 2d. Similarly, many employer meetings use call badges to find out traffic. If you are coming near a fixed cold, take a 2d to look over the names in advance than you stroll up. An extra few seconds of time spent actively focusing can be the difference amongst disaster and success. It moreover guarantees which you are not seeing the names for the primary time, in actual time.

When a pilot works in the course of their tool rating, they teach to fly through clouds, wherein visibility is regularly 0. They depend mostly on their instruments. Once the pilot is familiar with their devices, this isn't always specially difficult. This have to be rehearsed until the mechanics are 2nd nature, and the pilot knows the steps to comply with internal and out. Only then can all intellectual energy be spent following the instruments instead of figuring out a manner to interpret them.

Similarly, in case you are seeing names for the primary time and seeking to memorize them concurrently, it may display tough. By reviewing a visitor listing, analyzing name badges, or searching up convention attendees on LinkedIn previous to arrival, you could deliver your self a leg up that might make all the distinction.

WHEN YOU MEET SOMEONE

When you meet any character for the primary time, LISTEN! There is a marked difference between taking note of a call and absorbing the name into your mind. Memorizing names requires the latter. Actively repeat humans's names again to them, and then repeat the call internally. Don't allow the tray-passed hors d'oeuvres grow to be a distraction! One of my mentalist superpowers is assertion. As the pronouncing is going, we have been given ears and one mouth simply so we are capable of pay interest times as a good deal as we talk.

Chapter 15: Create A Caricature

Artificial intelligence does a amazing mission at mimicking fact. Deep-fake technology can create a automated vocal tune that appears like one in each of our favourite singers or possibly fabricate movies of our favourite celebrities. The BBC determined itself in a bit of warm water in 2020 after growing a faux Christmas message from the past due Queen Elizabeth II. Even even though it have come to be touted as fictitious through the network, humans had been concerned at really how convincing it seemed.

As correct as computers are at mimicking reality, they however war with facial popularity. Not the sort that unlocks our phones, wherein there may be a controlled environment and we're looking proper now at the display show screen. I'm talking approximately the sort in which they ought to choose human beings from a crowd right away. For a few motive, laptop structures battle to find out the maximum salient physical dispositions that make someone appear like themselves.

Everybody from law enforcement to AI specialists has have become to caricaturists to examine the manner they do what they do. Yes, the same shape of caricaturist who drew the embarrassing photograph of you at your final company tour party. Erik Learned-Miller of the Computer Vision Laboratory at the University of Massachusetts, Amherst, says that "the notable detail about cool lively film artists is that they may be capable of 0 in on the maximum one-of-a-kind element of someone." Learning to memorize names manner we must learn how to view human beings otherwise.

We all have comparable compositions. Two eyes above a nose above a mouth. We are all manner greater alike than we're different, that is one of the reasons that it's far much less complicated to distinguish among human beings we realize nicely. I understand a pair of identical twins, and it turn out to be only after approximately a month of hanging out with them frequently that I ought to tell them aside clearly as without troubles as I must spot my special buddies. Even despite the fact that they may be "equal," there are small bodily versions to be decided, no longer to mention versions of their demeanor and the way they invent themselves. A caricaturist can also select up on these versions, and you ought to too.

When you meet any person, ask your self how a caricaturist may also draw them. This can be a completely uncomfortable enjoy in case you are not used to it. We are all taught to be well mannered, and for absolutely everyone we meet whose maximum effective feature might be a chiseled face and robust jawline, there can be every one-of-a-kind who might also have a far much less flattering feature soar out at us. As we have been taught whilst we had been young, "Don't stare!" You ought that allows you to pick out out a prominent function short, and you can exercise with people you observe on TV or while you're out and about before you try it on the method.

Also, preserve in thoughts that your capability to memorize names will fast emerge as a few thing that others need to have a look at. Outside of suggesting this e-book, it might be realistic to hold your creative imagery to yourself. Just due to the fact some thing is a useful device does not recommend that everyone will want to recognize EXACTLY how you're picturing them to take into account their call.

Let's try some right now. Look over the photos beneath and spot if you could find a manner that you can in all likelihood caricature that character.

GRACE

Take a 2nd to anticipate via your first impressions. If you have been drawing a fab animated film of those three humans, what wouldn't it appear like? These are your very own thoughts and do not need to be shared with absolutely everyone, so supply your self the liberty to apply your creativeness.

Okay, is it completed? If you have not finished it however, I specifically advise which you take a moment to attempt right now. You will get manner greater out of trying this yourself than through absolutely studying my options.

When I have a look at Keith, the primary factor that I check is the shape of his hairline and the way it makes what nearly looks like a Batman logo. You may additionally as a substitute look at his beard right away, or possibly the caterpillar-like eyebrows. Like I mentioned earlier than, it may sense atypical to do that at the same time as, for max of our lives, we're educated not to interest an excessive amount of on bodily appearances. To try this nicely, it requires that we do the alternative of what we are used to, however preserve in thoughts that this is all about an goal method with a clean reason. In no way is it approximately making judgments!

When I actually have a observe Ashley, the thin, descending eyebrows are the number one element I look at. One may be aware about your flower headscarf and matching pinnacle, but be careful approximately selecting items or accessories on someone. If they change amongst conferences, your anchor will be misplaced at sea.

When I see Grace, I at once note the form of her smile. She seems welcoming and welcoming, and her cheeks body the smile nicely. That's in all likelihood the phase of her face that is probably the maximum memorable to me and what I would possibly spotlight if I made a caricature of her.

It is a long manner higher to pick out any characteristic than none in any respect, so don't worry in case your first few tries are difficult to don't forget. It gets much less difficult. I discover that there are extraordinary talents which can be a long way less complicated to keep in mind for me than others. The first locations I usually generally tend to look are constantly on their faces. It gives the maximum facts and is the least probably to exchange from everyday.

Just like a caricaturist begins offevolved through analyzing to draw a regular face, you can increase to start thinking about faces as rotating mixtures of capabilities.

Eyebrows and Eyes

Foreheads

Lips

Noses

Wrinkles / Lines

Moles / Beauty Marks / Dimples

If this appears overly simplistic to you, bear in mind that all sun shades are made from outstanding 3 number one sun shades. A beginning artist may additionally moreover simplest recognise a manner to make a single colour of green, however an established artist can differentiate among severa sun sun shades with out problem, at the side of or subtracting extra blue or yellow to collect the stop result they will be seeking out. Similarly, you turns into adept as noticing smaller nuances that you can have left out earlier than.

You can throw beards and facial hair inside the mixture as nicely, however the ones do no longer stick pretty as properly for me until they're very prominent capabilities (like Adam's beard). Accessories, like glasses and garb, are difficulty to alternate, so the ones may be risky to choose as an anchor. In a pinch, some difficulty is better than no longer something, so it's better to pick out

out any individual's glasses than to skip this step. At the very least, the greater effort positioned into noticing the individual will bypass an extended manner inside the course of remembering their name.

Keep in thoughts that those are designed to be transient places to hold statistics. Just like we do no longer want to apply these recommendations to endure in mind the names of close to friends and circle of relatives individuals, the stop intention is that finally the names we analyze become hard-coded into our memories thru repetition, and we're capable of ditch the mnemonics completely.

Remember that our on foot memory may be very restrained and may first-rate hold about seven devices MAXIMUM. This approach that if you meet four people and need to memorize their names, this is already a taxing burden to your mind's processing electricity except you operate a few kind of device. If you train your self to look for identifying functions, you are already a big leap beforehand, as you could higher proper now differentiate the human beings you meet.

Chapter 16: Choose A Code Word

Once you've got recognized a feature to CARICATURE, you're a 3rd of the manner via the 3Cs (don't forget: CARICATURE, CODE, CHANGE). The subsequent thing to do is to choose your CODE phrase.

Your code phrase may be a word which you use as a bridge over again to the call. Last chapter, we stated Adam and his beard, and used the code word APPLE as it made us consider an "Adam's Apple."

If you have got were given ever have a have a look at a few issue approximately mnemonics, you could have heard of the "reminiscence palace" technique. Essentially, it's far the concept of using a place nicely, like your home, to function as a preserving bay for statistics. Let's say which you want to shop for five grocery items at the shop: broccoli, milk, hen, yogurt, and flour. You may take an imaginary stroll through your private home and mentally pin items at diverse locations.

As people, we recall snap shots and testimonies higher than a few thing else. Even hundreds of years in advance than the written word, we exceeded on data via memories and imagery.

For example, as you walk up to your door, you can picture the doorknob as a massive head of broccoli. When you open the door, your children have hung a bucket of milk above you that splashes down in your head and soaks you. In my house, I might input a foyer, wherein there may be an oil portray of my partner and me that was a wedding present. In this case, our heads in the painting had been changed by manner of using chickens! I might then skip clockwise through the house. Notice that our piano is complete of yogurt, and the keys have have turn out to be to yogurt as nicely. It's no longer possible to play some factor with out getting sticky arms! Finally, I should see my eating table and look at that it changed into in reality covered in flour. We have cats, so

I might even see their little paw prints within the flour as they chased each other.

Was that smooth for you to photograph? You may additionally already be able to taking walks thru the grocery listing from reminiscence. Without searching lower lower back, what became the doorknob fabricated from? What happened while you opened the door? What about the big oil portray of me and my wife? And the piano? Finally, what approximately my consuming room desk? If you scored 5/five, congratulations. You're already a reminiscence professional! If you didn't score well, don't be discouraged. Instead, take a second to in truth visualize the imagery and strive all over again. By making the ones snap shots stick out in your mind, you will ultimately acquire achievement.

This leads us proper now decrease decrease returned to code phrases. You already understand what broccoli seems like, and maximum folks have a sizable photograph that includes mind. We want a unique option for a name because of the reality we do now not recognise specially what a "Mary" seems like. Or what exactly a "Brian" looks like. If we did, all Brians would appearance precisely the same, and there may be no want for this e-book. You should simply stroll proper into a room and be able to grow to be aware of all the Brians, all of the Marys, and lots of others. Simply as without problem as saying "That is a ebook" and "That is a desk." Remember that every one a mnemonic beneficial beneficial useful resource does is feature as a bridge leading from one piece of statistics to some distinct. The code word is the bridge. When I think about the decision Mary, the primary factor that includes mind is "Mary Had a Little Lamb." My code phrase for Mary is a lamb. For Brian, you may think of a thoughts, or perhaps of Brian, the anthropomorphic white canine from Family Guy.